Never
Blink in a
Hailstorm

and *Other Lessons*
on Leadership

Never
Blink in a
Hailstorm
and *Other Lessons*
on Leadership

David L. McKenna

BakerBooks
Grand Rapids, Michigan

© 2005 by David L. McKenna

Published by Baker Books
a division of Baker Publishing Group
P.O. Box 6287, Grand Rapids, MI 49516-6287
www.bakerbooks.com

Printed in the United States of America

Library of Congress Cataloging-in-Publication Data
McKenna, David L. (David Loren), 1929–
    Never blink in a hailstorm and other lessons on leadership / David L.
McKenna.
          p.   cm.
    Includes bibliographical references.
    ISBN 0-8010-6540-2 (pbk.)
    1. Leadership—Religious aspects—Christianity. I. Title.
BV4597.53.L43M45 2005
253—dc22   2004023175

To
Doug and Rob,
our sons
and my
colleagues in the field of organizational psychology;
partners in the matters of faith, mind, and spirit;
consultants in the study of creative Christian leadership

Contents

Acknowledgments

To *Jan, my wife of fifty-four years*, who knows that writing is my second love;

To *my mentors*, whom God placed at the intersections of my life to point the way and help me understand the "road not taken";

To *the members of my executive teams* at Spring Arbor University, Seattle Pacific University, and Asbury Theological Seminary, who made me look good, even when I didn't deserve it;

To *faculty scholars and teachers* at these institutions who dared me to think "otherwise";

To *Dwight Baker, Don Stephenson, and the staff of Baker Publishing Group*, who took a chance that this book has its own niche in a saturated field;

To *Aidan and Ryan*, our 11th and 12th grandchildren, whose simple faith and wide-eyed wonder prove that God has not given up on the world.

Preface

Our secular society suffers from a severe loss of memory. The loss is aggravated by a postmodern mind that honors neither history nor heroes. Leadership literature is an exception. Rather than limiting itself to theoretical research and social surveys, it fleshes out the meaning of leadership in the life stories of men and women who have learned the lessons of success and failure in a setting that exposes their humanity, tests their morality, and probes their spirituality. Even in secular leadership writing, words such as *commitment, values, character, trust,* and *humility* grace the pages to remind us of timeless truth and unforgettable people.

Memory serves as a motive for writing this book. Even if the current generation tends to neglect its history and its heroes, the record of the past needs to be preserved for the time when sound bites fade and celebrities fail. Unapologetically, I draw from my experience spanning fifty years in education, religion, and civic affairs with the hope that a new generation of Christian leadership will get a jump start on the future. Even though God has no grandchildren, the progressive revelation of his Word tells us that he believes in memory as a learning instrument.

I also write with the idea of mentoring in mind. Further credit goes to the genre of leadership literature for its adoption of mentoring as a way to connect the past with the future. By recognizing that past leaders have something unique to contribute to future leaders, mentoring is a direct repudiation of a secular and postmodern mind-set. I feel especially rewarded to see the process of mentoring go beyond a functional craft into a creative art. Any craftsman of leadership can speak eloquently about the style of administration that leads to effectiveness, but only an artist can communicate the spirit of leadership that leads to greatness. Just the fact that books on leadership acknowledge mentoring as a critical dimension of leadership development is a major gain for the past generation.

One of the unforgettable persons in my life is a Boeing engineer who is credited for the design of the "Flying Fortress," widely known as the aircraft that won World War II. The B-17 is also reputed to be the best-designed aircraft in the history of aeronautics. I came to be a friend of the designer, not by his aeronautics, but by his art. After his retirement, he began painting exquisite landscapes that sold for thousands of dollars. Enthralled by his artistry, I asked him how an engineer could become an artist. He responded by relating the discipline of aircraft design to the creative thrust of oil painting. "Once I obey the laws of aerodynamics for an airplane or the laws of form, line, and color for a painting," he explained, "I am set free to create the product of my imagination."

What profound truth! I discovered this same truth in my experience as a Christian leader. To be creative, we need freedom, and to be free, we need discipline. Isn't this the principle that Jesus gives us when he says, "You will know the truth, and the truth will set you free" (John 8:32)? Doesn't it also follow that Jesus's promise of the "fullness of life" is another way of expressing the artistry of creative Christian living? For me, the principle and the promise apply directly to Christian leadership. Discipline leads to freedom, and freedom opens the door to creativity. This is what I mean when I conclude this book with the chapter entitled "Free Indeed!" Artistry in Christian leadership is a present possibility for each one of us. To God be the glory!

David L. McKenna

1

When "No" Means "Go"

Leadership is an exhilarating experience. Like a sailor who is borne on the wings of the wind, a leader thrives on the freedom to cast visions, explore options, and take risks. Visionary leaders with an entrepreneurial spirit especially need freedom to exercise their gifts. When set free, they energize people and transform organizations. Max DePree has it right in the title of his book *Leadership Is an Art.*[1] Management is a science of learned skills; leadership is an art of intuitive sense. Management produces quantifiable results; leadership gives the added value of aesthetic quality. Like a concert pianist whose music soars with a spirit far beyond the notes on the printed score, leadership rises to art form when the spirit is free and beauty is seen.

"STOP" and "GO" Signs

Leaders are free only within limits. Legal, ethical, organizational, and positional boundaries are erected around the role of a leader. The leader cannot violate these boundaries without losing effectiveness and credibility. John Carver, in his book *Boards That Make a Difference,* gives us a memorable phrase that identifies these boundaries. An effective governing board, he says, will tell its chief executive officer, "GO until we say STOP."[2] Within these broad boundaries, the executive leader has the freedom to range far and wide over the organizational landscape in order to fulfill the vision, meet the mission, and grow the people with a touch of artistry. Quite the opposite, another governing board may tell its chief executive officer, "STOP until we say GO." This command draws such tight boundaries on leadership that freedom is severely limited and creativity is stifled. Good governance as well as full confidence are best expressed in the freedom within boundaries conferred by the statement, "GO until we say STOP."

When God Says "GO"

In the creation story, God gives Adam and Eve full freedom within broad boundaries for the leadership of the Garden of Eden. They are free to eat the fruit of any tree in the Garden except for the Tree of Life that stands at the center. By giving them this command, God is saying, "GO until I say STOP." The boundary is the Tree of Life, whose fruit represents the knowledge and wisdom of God himself. To eat of this tree is to tromp on turf that belongs to God alone. By living within this limit, however, Adam and Eve are set free to lead all creation in the use and development of its abundant resources. Full freedom within broad boundaries is evidence of God's personal relationship with Adam and Eve and his confidence in their leadership.

Consistent with his Garden command, God gives Moses ten commandments, eight of which begin with the negative, "You shall not . . ." For those who violate these commandments, the prohibitions are burdensome. But those who keep them have freedom to range far and wide in the affirmations of relationship with God, family, and neighbors. The Ten Commandments are the boundaries for freedom in a civilized society, not just in a Christian nation. If these boundaries are broken, human freedom must be restricted. If they are kept, people are set free.

Jesus also says, "GO until I say STOP" to his twelve disciples when he sends them out with full power and authority to preach his Word, heal the sick, and cast out demons. After giving them the freedom of "GO," he says, "STOP." Three limits are set. They are to: (1) take nothing for their journey; (2) stay in only one house; and (3) shake the dust off their feet if people of a village do not welcome them (Luke 9:1–6). Each of these limits makes sense. If they take a staff, a bag, money, and extra clothing with them, they will appear superior to the poor whom they are called to reach. If they stay in more than one house while visiting a town, they can be accused of playing favorites. If they let people's receptivity to the gospel influence their ministry, the truth may be compromised. Jesus knows from experience where the boundaries between freedom and failure lay for the future leaders of the church. By saying, "GO until I say STOP," he sets the limits without stifling our ingenuity for doing our primary task.

When Wisdom Says "NO"

What are the boundaries within which leaders find their freedom? Where are the stop signs erected for leadership? Some are pointed and direct; others are more subtle.

Returning to the thoughts of John Carver in his book *Boards That Make a Difference*, we discover the surprising statement that executive leaders should be subject to only two major limitations: prudence and ethics.[3] Prudence is the exercise of sound judgment in decision making; ethics are the moral standards of right and wrong against which the decisions are made. Stated in negative terms, Carver says a governing board must decide what it will not put up with. *"Don't do dumb things"* is the test of prudence. A university president who spends a million dollars to remodel the president's home fails at the point of prudence. *"Don't do wrong things"* is the test of ethics. The pastor who pads his expense account fails the test of ethics.

One of the earliest lessons I learned about the limits of leadership came from John W. Gardner, author of a classic book written a generation ago under the title of *Excellence*. Gardner gives his own working principle for the selection of leaders who will be excellent. He says to seek leaders for "taste and judgment. Almost everything else can be bought by the yard."[4] Stated negatively as boundaries for leadership, Gardner might say, *"Don't violate good taste"* and *"Don't neglect sound judgment."* These principles served me well during my years as a president in higher education who had the responsibility for selecting leaders for my administrative staff. By making observations about taste during the recruiting stage and creating case studies on judgment during interviews, I seldom chose wrong. Taste is tested by such factors as dress and demeanor. A woman who wears a miniskirt to interview for a position as executive assistant to the president or a man who is insensitive to racial and ethnic differences lacks good taste. Judgment is a test of practical wisdom in decision making. A candidate for a leadership position who trashes a former boss or tells what's wrong with the company before employment lacks good judgment. Whatever the position for which we are recruiting, the tests of taste and judgment serve us well.

Christian leaders join their secular colleagues in being subject to the limits of prudence and ethics. *"Don't do dumb things"* and *"Don't do wrong things"* are boundaries that no one can break under the guise of doing God's will. The same can be said for the principles about taste and judgment. There is no excuse for sloppiness in taste or shoddiness in judgment under the name of Christ. Excellence in Christian leadership begins within the limits of prudence and ethics, taste and judgment. But this is just the beginning.

When God Says "No"

Christian leaders also come up against the limits of their sacred calling. *"Don't do sinful things"* is the boundary within which Christian leaders find their freedom. When bishops of the early church were ordained, they took vows to be true to the Word of God and to live blameless in character. Negatively stated, they vowed never to teach heresy and never to live in sin. Within these broad boundaries, however, they were free to lead and serve. As simple as it sounds, Christian leaders of the past and present whom we extol as saints or models of the heart of Jesus Christ are those who serve with freedom between those boundaries. Equally simple, those who fall from grace are violators of one or the other of these limits on freedom.

We see these principles come into focus in Acts 6 when an internal conflict based upon ethnic differences threatens to destroy the unity of the infant Christian church. The apostles realize that they are neither called to be administrators nor gifted for executive tasks. To their credit, however, they do know the special qualities of leadership that are needed to resolve the conflict. Under the guidance of the Holy Spirit, they propose that seven deacons be elected as administrators for the church. They were to be men *with a good reputation, filled with the Holy Spirit, and known for their practical wisdom* (see Acts 6:3). These are the special criteria for leaders who have the difficult task of resolving conflict, especially when resources are short and ancient hostilities of ethnic origin lurk just beneath the surface. Not by accident, the job description for the deacons begins with *a good reputation*. Credibility of character, both in public and church circles, still serves as the entry point for leadership. *Practical wisdom*, then, is a quality that goes beyond the limits of prudence or sound judgment. It includes the ability to see the "big picture" within which decisions are made and to anticipate the consequences of the decisions. These qualities of leadership are not natural gifts. A good reputation results from being tested in the crucible of public scrutiny, and practical wisdom comes from the experience of success and failure. Even these qualities are not enough. To be fully effective, their good reputation and practical wisdom must be enhanced by the *filling of the Holy Spirit*. Permeating our character with the motive of love and helping us see the "big picture" are superlatives of the Spirit-filled life.

When Experience Says "Never"

Experience in leadership serves as its own testing ground for the limits of freedom. Beginning with the freedom given by God and the limits imposed by wisdom, an executive adds personal insights from day-to-day practice that fill out the STOP and GO story of effective leadership. Because these insights are so personal, they have a special influence upon shaping the character of a leader. Integrity is at stake if they are neglected, but artistry is in the making if they are fulfilled.

This book is about the freedom found within the limits of leadership learned from experience. Building upon Carver's primary principle of governance, "GO until I say STOP," a corollary principle is explored. "When 'NO' means 'GO'" may appear to be a paradox, but it is also a truth that sets the leader free. Nothing is worse than trying to lead when the boundaries are hidden or freedom is fuzzy. Disaster awaits the leader who is held accountable for hidden expectations. After thirty-three years as a chief executive officer, experience has taught me that some STOP and GO lessons can save new and developing leaders a lot of grief up front. Boldly, then, I declare them to be maxims created when experience says, "NEVER."

McKenna's Maxims

Each maxim of leadership in this book is grounded in both theory and practice. During the early years of my administrative career, I became a student of leadership in my graduate study. After taking courses in administrative theory, I chose to do my doctoral research in the field of leadership in higher education. At the age of 31, then, I was elected as the youngest college president in the nation. My baptism under fire put my academic preparation to test and made lifelong learning a survival tool. My education continued for a third of a century as I served as president of a college, a university, and then a theological seminary. Now, in retirement, I am asked to consult on presidential searches and coach developing leaders in both educational and religious organizations. In preparation for these assignments, I look back upon thirty-three years of experience in the chief administrative role to discover practical wisdom that has continuing value for leadership development. I often find myself surprised at the insights that come to me when asked for counsel on a specific problem. Almost as often I sense deep satisfaction when the insights make a difference in a leader's action and produce a small word of thanks.

The most gratifying of all of my coaching and consulting moments come when the lessons of experience are shared with Christian leaders who are motivated to follow the example of Jesus Christ and become totally dependent upon the resources of the Holy Spirit. Contrary to the opinion of some, the freedom of "GO" within the limits of "NO" is far greater for Christian leaders than for those who lead human organizations within the boundaries of the natural world. Colin Powell, Secretary of State under President George W. Bush, says, "Leadership is the art of accomplishing more than the science of management says is possible."[5] As this statement makes us consider leadership an art beyond the limits of science, it also prompts us to think about the potential of Christian leadership. Paraphrasing Powell's definition, we dare to say that "Christian leadership is accomplishing more with the power of the Holy Spirit than either the art or science of leadership says is possible." We must never forget that leaders who serve in the name of Jesus Christ and depend upon the Holy Spirit are agents of the supernatural and ministers of a kingdom larger than any human institution. For this reason alone, the degrees of freedom for leadership are multiplied. When Jesus says, "The truth will set you free," he opens up options for leadership that include the unlimited resources of the Father, the boundless promises of the Son, and the constant presence of the Holy Spirit. With a "NO" to self, we get a "GO" from God.

Each of the maxims of leadership presented in this book represents a co-mingling of administrative theory, executive experience, and spiritual lessons taught by the Holy Spirit. Admittedly, they pose a paradox between the discipline of "STOP" and the freedom of "GO." Paradox, however, is the stuff of which leadership is made. Danish physicist Niels Bohr, winner of the Nobel Prize in 1922, said of paradox: "How wonderful that we have met with a paradox. Now we have some hope of making progress."[6] Our "STOP" and "GO" maxims are offered with the same engaging spirit of inquiry. Paradox tells us that we are on to something.

2

Never Play God

Our maxims of leadership begin with the prohibition: "Never play God." Leaders who are vaulted to the pinnacle of power are particularly susceptible to the temptation to upstage God. If we succumb to this temptation, we will always crumble under the weight of our own ego as we pretend to have the power or the position of God. I am not talking about megalomaniacs like Alexander the Great, who wanted his visage carved into the side of a mountain in ancient Greece. Anyone who is a leader with followers is subject to the same temptation and sin that drove Adam and Eve out of the Garden. We want to be as wise as God by pretending to be competent, in control, and deserving credit for our accomplishments. Nothing is further from the truth.

Confusing Means and Ends

Christian leaders can inadvertently play God when we become victims of a "great distortion." Taking our cue from secular management, we focus upon results and judge our success by the "bottom line." A report of increased sales, an improved profit margin, and a greater return to the shareholders are evidence of success in secular leadership. To judge Christian leaders by the same or similar criteria is to distort the truth of the gospel and inadvertently play God. Nowhere in Scripture do we read that the disciples of Jesus Christ are either accountable for results or judged by their success. Quite to the contrary, they are judged only by their faithfulness to the message of the gospel and their modeling of the message in their personal life. Faithfulness, not success, is the criterion for the evaluation of Christian leaders.

When Jesus gives his disciples the Great Commission, he talks about means rather than ends. To *go* into all the world and *make* disciples of all nations, *teaching* them to obey his commandments are all the means, not the ends, of Christian leadership. If the Great Commission is taken literally, a great burden falls off the back of Christian leaders. We are accountable for the means of ministry, but not the ends of ministry. God himself accepts responsibility for the results.

In a public address, Senator Mark Hatfield tells of visiting Mother Teresa and asking, "How can you go out each morning to the streets of Calcutta and minister to the dying while knowing that you can never be successful?" Mother Teresa answered, "God did not call me to be successful. He only called me to be faithful."

Her response is consistent with everything we read in Scripture about the call of God for leaders. When Jesus calls his disciples, he invites them to "Come, follow me . . . and I will make you fishers of men" (Matt. 4:19). Again, the verbs *come*, *follow*, and *make* are means to the end of becoming fishers of men. Even then, fishing is a process. The catch belongs to God.

Skip forward in Scripture to Christ's promise about giving a glass of water in his name: "If anyone gives even a cup of cold water to one of these little ones because he is my disciple, I tell you the truth, he will certainly not lose his reward" (Matt. 10:42). Sure, a reward is promised, but its nature is not specified. His disciples are called to be "givers of water" from the motivation of love, not the expectation of a reward. The same principle carries over to the last judgment. God separates the sheep from the goats not according to the results of their earthly work but on the basis of their response to the hungry, thirsty, sick, naked, and imprisoned stranger (Matt. 25:31–46). In each case we are being introduced to the true meaning of unconditional love. Feeding the hungry, giving water to the thirsty, clothing the naked, welcoming the stranger, and visiting the prisoner cannot be a planned tactic with the results on a score sheet. Christian compassion rises from within and is as natural as breathing for those who have been redeemed by love. Not surprisingly, then, the sheep do not remember their acts of compassion, nor do the goats remember their failure to be compassionate. That which is natural to our character is also spontaneous, incidental, and often unconscious.

Christian leaders play God when we succumb to the temptation to substitute success for faithfulness. Like Roman legions parading slaves as proof of their victory, we are often guilty of playing the numbers game to prove our results. Taking our cue from the secular world, we use growth in numbers, dollars, and bricks as evidence of our success. When this happens, spiritual quality quickly gives way to three sins.

One is the *sin of competitive statistics*. Ironically, at the same time that we use a horizontal scale to assess the equal worth of every person in the sight of God, we counter it with a vertical scale for judging the success of Christian leaders in our denominations, local churches, educational institutions, missionary agencies, and social ministries. On a vertical scale, someone is always at the top and someone is always at the bottom. Currently, megachurches are at the top of a vertical scale of churches and setting the pace for all others to follow. The sheer number of pastors and church leaders who gather annually at conferences sponsored by megachurches tells the tale. Megachurches themselves are not at fault. Most of these churches' pastors work hard to avoid the image of being the model for all to follow. But built into any human system is that tendency to establish a pecking order with someone at the top. Add the fact that so many pastors and churches are frustrated by the failure to reach unbelievers and grow believers, and desperation leading to adulation and imitation is the natural response.

The *sin of cheapened means* follows. When the emphasis is upon competitive statistics as the goal of the church, the temptation is to cheapen the means of ministry. In their book *Blown to Bits*, Philip Evans and Thomas Wurster talk about tension in the goals of business enterprises between "reach" and "richness."[1] All businesses want to reach out and win new markets, but when they do, resources are stretched and the richness of quality and service is sacrificed. A similar pattern can be seen in churches. Reach usually means a sacrifice in richness. One church prides itself in the promise to eliminate the obstacles that keep nonbelievers away from church. To fulfill the promise, they downplay or eliminate traditional symbols, creeds, hymns, rituals, and sermons. In their place they build a theater-like sanctuary, play pop-style music, promise nonthreatening sermons, promote fairs and festivals, and offer a wide range of therapeutic groups for every relational need. While their reach may sound as if it has a richness to it, the soft underbelly of ministry is evident in the high turnover of attendees, the sharp fallout of members, and the failure to nurture youth through to spiritual maturity. Of course, this is not just the fault of churches that are trying to keep step with the megachurch mentality. The traditional church itself can be faulted for professing to assure richness in ministry while failing to reach the lost of its own community. Perhaps both extremes are victims of a vertical mentality of competition between churches. Contemporary churches err on the side of reach, and traditional churches err on the side of richness. Neither one offers the complete ministry needed in a world spinning out of control.

Churches are not alone in committing the sin of cheapened means. As a longtime consultant for Christian colleges and universities, I have seen endless examples of educational decisions based upon the "cash cows" of cheapened programs. One board of trustees arbitrarily ordered the establishment of a school of business in order to capitalize on the popularity of the program in the student marketplace. Another institution risked its reputation for quality by taking on a questionable degree-completion program in a distant city with the hope of a quick return in revenues. The list can go and on. Meanwhile, many businesses will cheapen their product or utilize foreign sweatshops in order to undercut their competitors and increase their profit. The temptation is endemic to leadership in a competitive climate.

The sins of competitive statistics and cheapened means lead inevitably to the *sin of stolen glory*. Leaders have a hard time pretending to be humble when they want to take the credit for their achievements. They quote the adage, "It doesn't matter who gets the credit if the work gets done," but it rings hollow. They extol the work of their followers, but no one believes them. Some even go so far as to give God the glory, but it sounds insincere. In one way or another, leaders who are playing God with means and ends will betray their love for self-glory. When talking about their achievements, their favorite word is "*I*." When counting their accomplishments, their favorite exhibit is a press clipping. Self-made leaders who have risen from the lowest ranks are particularly susceptible to this temptation. Like the new rich who have had a meteoric rise into wealth, newcomers to success in leadership feel a need to show off their achievements. Our problem begins when we try to play God.

Counting on Our Competence

At the age of twenty-one, I took my nineteen-year-old bride to a small parish in Vicksburg, Michigan, where I served as pastor while completing my bachelor's degree at Western Michigan

University. Shortly after we arrived, our conference superintendent called a meeting of ministers to set our goals for the year. He opened the retreat with the question, "What in the world are you doing that you could not do without the help of the Holy Spirit?" No one missed his point. Our competence as Christian leaders can get in the way of our dependence upon God and the work of his Holy Spirit.

The superintendent's question has stayed with me through the past fifty years. Coming from a home where neither parent graduated from high school, I developed an insatiable thirst for learning. Degrees in history, theology, counseling psychology, and higher education administration prepared me for the presidency in Christian higher education. Even during my career, my pursuit of greater competency continued. Study in strategic planning, campus master planning, curriculum development, capital campaigns, faculty growth plans, student life assessment, and the integration of faith and learning all became additions to my professional portfolio. Later I used my experience to gain competence in consulting and teaching on the development of governing boards, presidential searches, and leadership theory. Henri Nouwen would say that my knapsack was filled with competencies.[2] One might expect that I had an answer for every question, a tool for every task, and a remedy for every ill.

The test of time proves otherwise. The more dependent I am upon my competencies, the less dependent I am on God. Nouwen's book *In the Name of Jesus* brings me up short every time I read it. Recounting his transition from the academic community of Harvard with the best and the brightest students to the pastoral community of Daybreak with its developmentally disabled residents, he likens himself to an onion being stripped of the layers of competence until only his naked self remains. At the core of his being, he finds himself deficient. When the residents of Daybreak look at him with the question in their eyes, "Do you love me?" Nouwen learns why God called him to Daybreak with the promise, "Go among the poor in spirit and they will heal you." Unconditional love is the ultimate competency for Christian leadership. It cannot be earned by degrees, conferred through titles, given with awards, or written in books. Competency in unconditional love comes only through utter dependence upon God.

I am still learning this lesson. Competency of function is my strength; competency of spirit is my weakness. Dependence upon competency is my temptation; dependence upon God is my thirst.

Claiming to Be in Control

Power and control are dirty words in the literature on Christian leadership. This is a bad rap because power and control cannot be dissociated from effective leadership. If power is the ability to influence the behavior of followers, Jesus is the most powerful leader in human history. Likewise, if control is the ability to determine destiny, he stands alone in this category of leadership. Writers such as Henri Nouwen and Max DePree do not serve us well when they write about leadership without power. Power is a neutral agent that can be used for good or evil, depending upon the mission and motivation of the user. Control can be equally good or evil. If any elements stand on the razor's edge of responsibility for Christian leadership, power and control are the first to qualify. They are primary tools in our downfall when we try to play God.

We must begin with the confession that most leaders are control freaks. We use diverse tactics to put ourselves in charge. I remember with a chuckle the disarming way in which Hugh White, chairman of the board of trustees at Spring Arbor College when I was president, took control. When engaged in debate with theologians or educators, he would listen to the discussion and then enter by saying, "I am just a simple layman and I don't quite understand the question." Using lay language and often punctuating it with his knowledge of accounting practices and tax law, Hugh White would remake the case and usually win his way.

Charles Odegaard, president of the University of Washington, had his own tactic as a prominent medieval historian. Whenever I heard him speak before the state legislature or at educational gatherings, I knew that he was taking charge with the introduction, "My field is medieval history, and it may have something to say to us today." As the mantle of his authority fell over the session, he pressed his case to a conclusion favoring his position.

I too am a control freak. Throughout my executive career, I prided myself on the fact that I controlled the direction of the institutions that I led. Some subordinates accused me of being authoritarian, and I am sure that I was on occasion. But generally speaking, I preferred to be known as an authoritative leader who used vision and intellect to anticipate issues and make informed decisions. This was my way of being in control. If I can get a grip on issues, I have the confidence that I can bring them to resolution. Without that point of control, however, I feel frustrated and on the edge of panic.

A prime example is my penchant for perfectionism in public speeches. As a high school debater and college speech teacher, I created a pattern of perfectionism against which I judged every speech or sermon. Before long, I suffered from what I call PMS—"Post-Message Syndrome." Lying awake at night, I gave the speech all over again, beating myself up for the things I had failed to say and wishing that I could take it back. More often than not, I needed a day or two to get over the sense of failure.

My release came from Fred Smith Sr., a wise mentor in management with a delightful sense of humor. When I started browbeating myself in Fred's presence for a speech that I had given, he took the occasion to tell me a story that illustrated his confidence in the sovereignty of God. While giving a speech, he took his house keys out of his pocket and threw them to a person sitting on the front row, saying, "Here are the keys to my house. I am giving it to you." Then he pretended that a phone rang and he answered it, "Hello. Yes, this is Fred Smith. My house has burned down? Too bad, I just gave it away."

"That's the way I approach a speech," Fred said. "After doing my best in preparation and in presentation, I give it to God and let him take care of the consequences." Fred's illustration brought to completion the admonition about preaching that I had heard in seminary. "Read yourself full, pray yourself hot, and preach yourself empty" now included the conclusion, "give yourself to God." Although I still have to double-check on my tendency for perfection, no longer do I find it necessary to play God. Exhilarating freedom comes with the knowledge that I have done my best in preparing and presenting a speech that is given to God. The greatest joy comes years after the speech is given and someone still remembers what was said with a life-changing effect.

Giving up control goes far beyond speech making. As executive leaders, even in the context of Christian ministry, we live with the temptation to run the world. It is a dangerous tendency in the office and a greater danger in the home. For me, home is the place where I learn humility. Even during the years when I was a college, university, and seminary president, our children were never awed. A younger daughter came home from school after learning about U.S. presidents to ask, "Daddy, President Eisenhower is famous. You are a president too. Why aren't you famous?" On another occasion I tried to use my executive authority to give an order to an older daughter. Without blinking, she openly defied me, and a family crisis followed. Because we are both bull headed, it was a standoff until I realized that I was treating her like a chattel slave and needed to ask her forgiveness.

The apostle Peter also tried to run the world. With his take-charge attitude and his obsession with control, he plays God time and time again throughout the Gospels. With the arrest of Jesus, however, his weakness is exposed in betrayal. Restoration doesn't occur until after the resurrection, when

Jesus asks him three times, "Do you love me?" Henri Nouwen interprets those three questions in the light of the temptations that are unique to Christian leaders—to be relevant, to go solo, and to be in control.[3] Like us, Peter succumbs to all three temptations, but his need to run the world is his undoing. To cure this tendency to play God, Jesus reminds him that as a young man, Peter was in full control, dressing himself and going where he wanted to go. Soon, however, he will be old and out of control. Someone else will dress him and take him where he does not want to go. This is Jesus' way of telling him that God alone is in control and Peter's destiny is a cross. With one last gasp of aggression, Peter looks at the disciple John and asks, "What about him?" Pointedly, Jesus responds, "What is that to you? Follow me" (see John 21:15–22). The command applies to every Christian leader. We must give up control and let God run the world.

In my retirement, Jesus' command to Peter comes back to me more times than I want to admit. No longer at the point of executive control, I see things that I do not like about the direction being taken by today's leaders of the evangelical community, the institutional church, and Christian higher education. My critical eye also faults the shallow writing on leadership theory, the pulp of some Christian fiction, the failure of social compassion and justice among believers, and the lack of imagination for a global church. On and on I could go, but every time I want to whine, complain, or protest, the Spirit of Jesus Christ pulls me up short with the command, "What is that to you? Follow me." Slowly and painfully, I am learning a lesson of spiritual maturity that comes with age. We have all we can do to manage ourselves and put ourselves in the hands of the One who leads us as he will and where he will. Now I know what Henri Nouwen means when he writes that all who serve in the name of Jesus must ultimately go from "leading to being led."[4]

Playing God is a never-ending temptation for Christian leaders. Either we obey the checks of the Holy Spirit when he calls this temptation to our attention or we replay the consequences of Adam's sin. By following the maxim "Never play God," we set ourselves free to explore a landscape of creative options and tap the full range of resources that God has given to us in his creation. When we let God be God, we who lead become the led.

3

Never Blink
in a Hailstorm

If you can't stand loneliness, stay away from leadership. Outside observers usually see the gregarious side of leaders. Standing out in the midst of a crowd, a leader attracts attention, commands respect, and relishes the presence of colleagues, staff, friends, and well-wishers. To say that a leader is lonely appears to be a contradiction in terms.

President Lyndon Johnson set the record straight in his common and crusty way. He said that being a leader was often like being a jackass in a Texas hailstorm—"You just have to stand there, close your eyes, and take it." Every leader knows what he means. It is lonely at the top when the buck stops and the hail cuts loose.

The Loneliness of Authority

The feeling of isolation may come from the authority involved in executive decisions. When Abraham Lincoln had to make an appointment from among ten nominees, he said that his decision resulted in nine enemies and one ingrate. Billy Martin, coach of the New York Yankees, left us a similar thought when he described a successful baseball manager as one "who keeps the five who hate you away from the four who are still unsure."

I learned the lesson of loneliness on the first day of my first presidency. Having served in the same college as a professor, dean, and vice president, I often walked home from the office with a faculty colleague who lived on the same street. After my first day in the office as president, the faculty member and I crossed paths on the campus and walked home together. Following the pattern of the past, we made small talk about people and events at the college. The next day, I learned my lesson. One of my "innocent" comments about plans for the college came back to me in the form of official policy. From then on I guarded my words, and by doing so I climbed a rung on the ladder of loneliness.

Former friends who became subordinates with my appointment as president do not understand this dilemma of leadership. When I began my third presidency, a longtime friend also served as a distinguished professor in the institution. He first approached me to say, "Let's get together once a week so that we can talk." As much as I appreciated him as a friend of proven worth, I had to say no. For one thing, I knew his reputation in faculty debates. He often played the devil's advocate in order to stir the pot of lively debate. He also was known for pontificating on selected issues. So as I declined his offer, I added, "Long ago, I learned that I must be president of all of the faculty. Authority turns friends into associates." He countered immediately with the argument that it was different for Christian brothers. "Secular institutions may draw these distinctions," he protested, "but in a Christian institution, we are all one." In faith, he spoke the truth, but in function, he was dead wrong. Christian faith does not blur the lines of authority or accountability for leaders. It does, however, infuse them with the qualities of truth and grace.

The lesson came home when I had to deal with that same faculty member after he had a heated confrontation with another colleague. Bringing a needed measure of objectivity to the conflict, I could tell him straight out, "You are wrong."

The Loneliness of Decision Making

I had to finalize my decision to distance myself from faculty friends during my second presidency. We had moved across a continent, leaving family behind. Naturally we needed friends with whom we could socialize. The director of athletics and his wife gave us a rare match of common interests for both my wife and me. During the transition period we were often together, relaxing and avoiding college talk. Our balloon of friendship was punctured by the first budget cycle of my administration. I had inherited an institution in financial trouble. Deep budget cuts had to be made. After working through the planning process and making the tougher decisions that are reserved for the president, I presented the budget to the campus community. Within minutes, word came back that another department head complained that athletics was favored because of my friendship with the director. Although the complaint contradicted the facts, I learned that perception carries a reality that cannot be denied. In such cases, no amount of explanation will make a difference. As painful as it was, my wife and I adjusted our social contacts within the faculty and found ourselves drawn more and more toward our immediate family. Time itself limited the cultivation of new friendships outside the institution. We felt loved, but lonely.

The Loneliness of Confidentiality

The analogy of the jackass in a Texas hailstorm takes on full meaning when an executive leader must make a controversial decision while holding in confidence the reasons behind the decision. The integrity of the institution, an individual, or a family is usually at stake.

Sooner or later, every executive leader will encounter moral issues that cannot be escaped. They may involve the makings of sexual scandal. Rumors come from credible sources who ask that confidentiality be held while expecting aggressive action. In such cases, the executive leader must decide whether or not to pursue the rumor or confront the subject. Patience is the course of wisdom, and confidentiality is its lonely partner. Early on, I determined that my job description did not include being a sleuth digging for dirt. Even now I recall rumors that I heard about faculty and staff that were plausible but unconfirmed. Right or wrong, I chose not to follow them because sleuthing can quickly become a full-time job.

The loneliness of leadership increases when the reports of moral problems are confessed or confirmed. Justice and mercy are then put on the scales with redemption as the balanced outcome. To tip the scale heavily toward justice or mercy is the easy way out. To balance them in decision making is far more difficult but nothing like the wrenching pain of redemptive action. Anyone who mouths the platitudes of cheap grace has never been in the shoes of an executive leader in a Christian organization. We preach redemption fluently, but we practice it only at a personal cost. I recall more than one incident in which a respected and visible faculty member was accused of moral failure. Each case ended up on my desk for a decision. Right or wrong, I called the person into the office to hear their version of the story. If I heard confession and contrition, another dilemma was forced upon me. I could make it a public case with ripple effects throughout the institution, the community, and the constituency, or I could take the route of rehabilitation with confidentiality for the sake of the individual and the family as well as the institution. Whenever possible, the latter is the course that I have taken. On two occasions, the price has been high. One spouse stormed into my office charging me with false accusations against her husband. Another spouse got wind of the rumor and indicted me for not letting her know what I had heard. In each case, I made the decision to protect the injured spouse and family. In the first case, the couple broke apart later on grounds of incompatibility. In the second case, the couple is still together with the family intact. A .500 batting average is sometimes the best that we can do.

Even more difficult have been decisions to preserve the integrity of the institution at the price of public misunderstanding. In my first presidency, we were "on the bubble" of accredited status between being a junior college and developing into a four-year liberal arts college. Faculty qualifications, especially the percentage of Ph.D.'s, were critical to achieve this goal.

In preparation for accreditation at the higher level, I turned the responsibility for the college's self-study over to a bright, young faculty member with Ph.D. credentials who had a gift for eyeballing educators and wowing students. In the middle of the process, an ugly truth came out. The young professor had falsified his academic credentials! Feeling betrayed by the one whom I had chosen as a future leader, I called him into my office for the inevitable confrontation. After he confessed his violation of professional ethics, I gave him the choice of resigning or being fired. He chose to resign, but not without a flourish. I bit the bullet while he went ahead with his announcement of resignation and I carried the shadow of having lost one of our best and brightest. As a thirty-three-year-old president, I had to appear before the faculty and student body to inform them of the resignation without revealing any other details. Afterward, I had to make the trip to the offices of the accrediting association and inform them that the self-study we had submitted included false information about the faculty credentials of the person who had coordinated the report. Quick action and open admission saved the day, but not without a painful lesson for a young president.

Perhaps the loneliest moment of all is reserved in the documents marked "CONFIDENTIAL: TO BE OPENED ONLY BY THE CHAIR

OF THE BOARD OR THE PRESIDENT" that are still sealed and secreted in the safe of an institution where I have served. No one knows their contents except the individuals involved and me. If revealed, they would damage the credibility of esteemed institutions, split families, and ruin legendary reputations. In each case, I made a choice. Perhaps it is because I remember the words of Carlyle when he witnessed a raucous mob celebrating a public hanging: "Except for the grace of God, there go I." Or perhaps it is because I believe in forgiveness for all who repent of their sin. Like a jackass in a Texas hailstorm, I closed my eyes and took it when the tough decisions came. Loneliness in leadership may well be the price for redemptive action.

Jesus Christ is the example beyond all examples of loneliness in leadership. We remember his ultimate loneliness on the cross when he cried out, "My God, my God, why have you forsaken me?" (Mark 15:34), but we may forget the background against which that cry was heard. Jesus appointed his twelve disciples not just to preach the Good News, heal the sick, and cast out demons but also "that they might be with him" (Mark 3:14). Like us, Jesus needed friends for support as he faced the loneliness of leadership. The fact that they all abandoned him when he went to the cross tells us what to expect when we make critical decisions that are misunderstood even by our friends. Unlike us, however, Jesus also knew what it meant to feel abandoned by God himself. As lonely as we may be in our leadership role, we will never know the isolation of God forsaking us. Our loneliness is real, but it is never ultimate. Christ is with us.

4

Never Go Solo

Leaders are often lonely, but they must never go it alone. This is not a contradiction. Loneliness is an occupational hazard of leadership that comes with the territory. Going solo is a conscious choice. Perhaps, as the flip side of loneliness, a leader with power and position begins to feel indispensable and untouchable. The temptation is to escape the check and balance of accountability to colleagues, community, and God himself. It is a dangerous moment. Confiding in no one, confessing to no one, and accepting criticism from no one, sin stalks the soloist.

Any leader who experiences loneliness will be tempted to go solo. Why trust people who will betray you? Why share confidential information with people who want your job? Why involve people who do not understand what it means to be lonely at the top? Any number of good reasons can be given for a leader to go solo.

Henri Nouwen, in his book *In the Name of Jesus*, confronts this question face to face.[1] After spending years as a distinguished professor in great universities, he realized that the natural forces of the academy were driving him to become more and more independent. Scholars dissociate themselves from colleagues in order to establish their own academic reputations. Authors of scholarly work seek first position on the listing in academic journals. Nobel prizes are given to individuals who stand out among their peers.

Professors and scholars are not alone in the temptation to go solo. Natural forces in every secular organization push the leader toward independence and isolation. When accountability is determined by speed of action, efficiency of operation, and measurable results, a leader can best achieve these goals by going it alone.

Christian leadership has to be different. Nouwen puts truth in a capsule when he writes, "When I go solo, I find it hard to be faithful."[2] He is confessing what most of us keep silent. Whether driven by an exaggerated ego or wounded pride, every Christian leader knows the temptation to go solo. We also know that Nouwen is right. When we are on our own, assuming to be accountable to no one except ourselves, it is hard to be faithful. To resist the temptation we need a critic, a confidant, and a community.

The Need for a Critic

Sometime during the 1970s, evangelical Christianity moved from a minor role to a major part in the drama of our culture. With visibility came vulnerability. Evangelical Christians learned what it meant to be under the klieg lights of the media. Billy Graham's words spoken in confidence to Richard Nixon about Jews in the media now come back to bite him a generation later. Jerry Falwell trips over his tongue so many times that even the most conservative of Christians want to distance themselves from his views. Jim Bakker pays the punishment for fraud in a jail cell. Ponzi schemes engineered by Christian leaders in the name of charity bilk aged and innocent believers out of millions of dollars. The list could go on and on, deeper and deeper, until the story involves scores of regional and local leaders, perhaps even to those of us who never make the headlines.

Can any common denominator be found for these defections and downfalls? Two personal lessons from experience point toward an answer. Years ago, I became intrigued by a book written by Robert Townsend, founder of Avis Rental Cars, titled *Up the Organization*. While Townsend's message centers upon the Japanese economic victory following military defeat, he makes a comment about leadership that has had a lasting impression on me. Townsend writes that every leader needs someone who can say, "No." To drive home his point, he uses Billy Graham as an example. He suggests that Graham's soul is saved, figuratively speaking, by T. W. Wilson, the only one of Billy's evangelistic team who could counter his unchecked ideas with the words, "Billy, that's B.S."[3] Even with barnyard language, the truth is not lost. Christian workers who go solo without the check and balance of someone who can say "No" are courting trouble.

Townsend's lesson is reinforced by Fred Smith Sr., one of my esteemed mentors. Sometime around 1978, when televangelism was at its height, Fred paid personal visits to the leaders of these ministries. Afterward, with the wry wisdom for which he is known, Smith summed up what he observed during his visits by telling me, "Dave, I can give you the names of those who will get in trouble. They are the ones to whom no one can say 'No.'" A few years later, I double-checked the names of the televangelists he mentioned. Fred was 100 percent right!

The Need for a Confidant

As an antidote to loneliness, leaders need someone in whom they can confide. With their superiors, they have to be performing artists; with their peers, they have to be insatiable optimists. With whom can they be themselves? Our son Doug is a consultant to executives who have either reached the top or are on the way. He has concluded that their greatest need is to confide in someone with whom they have total trust and can share their weaknesses. Christian leaders are no different. In leadership conferences for pastors, I have asked for a show of hands for those who have someone outside the church and their family in whom they can confide. Only a smattering of hands is raised.

I learned my lesson late in my career. While serving as president of Asbury Theological Seminary, I invited Dr. Lloyd Ogilvie to speak at our annual minister's conference. He came to the meetings as a Presbyterian among Methodists. After his first message, however, no one could doubt the size of his pastoral heart and the reach of his biblical message. In fact, after the first session, he asked me if it would be appropriate to give an altar call. Of course I said, "Yes, we are people who are open to the leading of the Holy Spirit."

In his final address, Dr. Ogilvie spoke on the subject of the refiner's fire. At the conclusion, the chapel air hung heavy with the sense of lonely and discouraged pastors needing the healing touch of God. Dr. Ogilvie asked for thirty pastors who were hurting to come forward and stand at the altar. Spontaneously, pastors stood and began to move forward. More than thirty lined up at the altar facing Ogilvie. He asked the congregation to bow in prayer while he heard the confession of each of the thirty pastors. Then, one by one, he put his hands on them and prayed for their healing. Time stood still as the sanctuary was filled with the presence of God. After praying with each one, Ogilvie asked them to turn and face the congregation as "wounded healers" who were now ready to hear the confession of others and pray for their healing. The aisles now filled as pastors and spouses formed lines in front of their supplicants.

Two and one-half hours after the service began, the last prayer was said. The picture of Dr. Lloyd Ogilvie himself standing alone with his hands on the head of the last pastor who had come forward is still etched in my mind. He missed his flight back to California in order to show us what it means to be a "pastor to pastors."

After the service, I invited Dr. Ogilvie to join me and Dr. Frank Bateman Stanger, my predecessor in the presidency at Asbury, for lunch. The three of us sat in the president's dining room, eating and reflecting on the service of the morning. After dessert, Dr. Stanger surprised us by saying, "Lloyd, you asked for hurting pastors to come forward this morning. I didn't come but I needed to. You see, earlier this morning my doctor told me that I have prostate cancer that has spread to the spine. I am hurting." Propelled from his seat, Lloyd Ogilvie dropped to his knees at Dr. Stanger's side and motioned me to kneel on the other. All three of us wept through Ogilvie's prayer for our esteemed brother. Frank Bateman Stanger, one of the best-known teachers and authors on the subject of healing, showed that none of us can go solo. Hesitant about going forward as president emeritus of the seminary and an authority on healing, he needed someone before whom he could reveal his deepest fears and anxiety.

After lunch, Lloyd Ogilvie came to my office where I too blurted out the truth that I was wounded and needed healing. This time he did not immediately pray for me. Instead, he said, "Dave, I too am wounded with no one to tell. Let's you and I become covenant brothers, keeping in regular contact to share our hurts and pray for our healing." In that moment, an eternal bond was formed between the two of us. We called each other regularly for years. My retirement and Lloyd's appointment as chaplain of the United States Senate stopped the calls, but the bond is still strong. Each of us knows that any time we need a confidant, no matter how grievous the confession or how dire the crisis, all other business will be put aside in order to answer a covenant brother.

Long before I learned this lesson, the writer of the book of Ecclesiastes said, "Two are better than one, because they have a good return for their work: If one falls down, his friend can help him up. But pity the man who falls and has no one to help him up! . . . Though one may be overpowered, two can defend themselves" (Eccles. 4:9–10, 12). The wisdom of the ancients speaks loud and clear to each of us, "Never go solo."

5

Never Steal
a Paper Clip

Among my mentors, I remember Kelly Waller, a tall Texan who never lost his drawl or his penchant for telling stories to get his point across. Kelly excelled as an insurance salesman. His last call to me came after his health had failed and his memory had slipped. With faltering voice and short-term memory, he still gave me his sales pitch.

Kelly's passion for sales took him from the ranks of a door-to-door salesman to the presidency of Safeco Growth Insurance Company, one of the largest in the world. After his retirement, he gave himself to leadership projects in the Seattle community, Rotary International, and a regular schedule of luncheons with young people whom he identified as future leaders of the community. In my role as the president of Seattle Pacific College (now University) at the age of thirty-nine, Kelly took me on. In our first luncheon together, he said that he had a story he wanted to tell me. "This is the story about a paper clip," he began. With that intriguing start, he spun his yarn.

When Kelly first joined Safeco as a rookie salesman, he was required to attend an orientation session keynoted by the chairman of the corporation. The chairman's speech always began by recounting the story of a young salesman who immediately caught the eye of his superiors as a potential leader for the company. While serving his apprenticeship, however, he was known as the guy who stocked his home office with supplies from the corporation, beginning with paper clips. As he climbed the corporate ladder, he took every advantage of the perks of his position, including padding his expense account. Still, nothing stopped him on his climb, and he attained the position of president. But with the power came exposure. Using corporate slight of hand, he negotiated a deal with a competitor that undermined his own company while giving him the advantage of new power, wealth, and position. Only an alert board of directors intercepted the move and saved the day. Their first act was to fire the president who had shown so much promise.

Concluding his story to the new recruits, the chairman of the board pressed home his point: "Never steal a paper clip."

Pennies and Paper Clips

Twice in my presidential career of thirty-three years my job was in jeopardy. One time involved a conflict with the board of trustees over the direction of the institution; the other time proved to be a test of my integrity. Information came to me that a colleague and longtime friend had failed to pay a debt due to the institution for a subsidiary enterprise that he led. Investigation showed that the funds had been collected but used for an investment with the hope of multiplying the resources in order to pay the debt and enhance the program. The investment had failed, and the debt was due.

Right or wrong, I decided to confront the person as my first course of action. In no uncertain terms, I laid down the ultimatum that the debt had to be paid within the next six weeks, before the books were closed on the fiscal year. If the debtor failed to make the payment, I would have no recourse but to make it an issue involving the board of trustees. This was my error. The same source that informed me of the debt also made an "end run" around me and informed the chairman of the board. The information triggered actions based upon mistrust. Assuming that I colluded with the colleague by failing to report the problem, an independent auditor was engaged to scrutinize all of my transactions as president, with a laser beam focused upon my expense accounts.

I knew nothing about the investigation until the chairman of the board asked to meet with me. In a confrontational setting, he raised questions about my relationship with the colleague, corrected me for not consulting him, and told me about the results of the independent auditor. A thorough scrutiny of all of my expense reports revealed no irregularities except a $28 expense for a baby mattress for the President's Retreat House at an off-campus site. When I told him that this expense was incurred for the purchase of a mattress for the baby bed that my wife and I had donated to the house so that a new administrator and his family could attend the annual retreat, he immediately relented. The most thorough audit had failed to produce one penny of misspent money. Admittedly, I had taken the issue with the colleague into my own hands and failed to notify the board, but not for fraudulent reasons. If a paper clip had been missing, I would have lost my job.

Later, Kelly Waller told me another sad story about a candidate for the presidency of a Seattle bank. He came through the search process far ahead of his competitors. Just before the announcement that he had been chosen as president, a final reference check was made on his academic credentials. He had claimed to hold a bachelor's degree in finance from a distinguished institution. The reference check proved otherwise. He had falsified his credentials! Without hesitation, the bank board canceled their invitation to him and chose the number two candidate. Kelly then made his point: "The saddest part is that the number two candidate did not hold a bachelor's degree either. If the first candidate had been honest, he would have had the job."

Visible and Vulnerable

Christian leaders are particularly vulnerable to the test of integrity. The more visible we are, the more vulnerable we are. Billy Graham, for instance, may be the most scrutinized Christian leader of our generation. His words, whether spoken from the crusade platform, in press conferences, at personal interviews, or during state visits, are all subject to the glaring light of media attention and public opinion. Late in his life he has been criticized for statements captured on tape during a conversation with Richard Nixon. His unmistakable voice is heard confirming the President's anti-Semitic remarks about the Jewish "stranglehold" upon American media. He even added, "They're the ones putting out the pornographic stuff." When the confidential tape was made public from the Nixon files, Graham said that he could not remember saying those words, but he immediately admitted that he was wrong in not disagreeing with the President, apologized to the Jews, and assured everyone that he no longer felt that way. One can envision Billy Graham, the North Carolina farm boy, being seduced by the power of the Oval Office and for a moment losing the prophetic voice that would have dared to refute the president of the United States. If we are honest, each of us has to admit that we too have our point of weakness. Unless we are on guard, the seduction of money, sex, or power can be our downfall.

Honest and Humble

Billy Graham survives in crisis because of his honesty and his humility. Most important is the fact that he models his own message of confession and forgiveness. Here is where Christian leadership differs from secular leadership. After news of the Watergate break-in hit the press, Richard Nixon chose to stonewall the facts and lie about his involvement. Insiders say that if he had confessed his wrong, the people would have forgiven him and he would have finished out his presidency. Instead, Nixon chose to cover up the facts and his part in the plot. Graham, in contrast, confessed that he was wrong, repented of his words, asked forgiveness, and disciplined himself by limiting the subject of any presidential audience to prayer and spiritual counsel. Of course, as *The Boston Globe* claimed, he "missed a powerful teaching moment, an opportunity to witness to the truth in the presence of a delusional leader."[1] But the important question is whether the evangelist acknowledged his part in this show of prejudice and learned from the experience. Graham's apology is a lesson for all leaders. He said, "As I reflect back, I realize that much of my life has been a pilgrimage—constantly learning, changing, growing and maturing. I have come to see in deeper ways some of the implications of my faith and message, not the least of which is the area of human rights and racial and ethnic understanding. Racial prejudice, anti-Semitism, or hatred of anyone with different beliefs has no place in the human mind and heart."[2]

Every leader is subject to the kind of temptation faced by Billy Graham. The more visible we are, the more vulnerable we are. In fact, leadership has its own unique set of occupational hazards for sin and wrongdoing. In the Old Testament, God warns kings about putting their trust in horses, treasures, and harems. The horses represent power; the treasures represent money; and the harems represent sex. Richard Foster has it right when he entitles his book *Money, Sex, and Power* as the domains of downfall for Christian leaders.[3] Like the stolen paper clip, the sin of money may begin with a padded item on an expense report; the sin of sex may begin with a flirtatious glance; and the sin of power may begin with an arrogant decision.

We expect Christian leaders to model their message. Sometimes we forget what the message includes. None of us is perfect, but all of us can be authentic. When the New Testament uses the Greek word for "sincere" to describe the servant of Jesus Christ, a picture appears before us. In the ancient Middle Eastern marketplace, the quality of pottery was tested by holding the item up against the bright sunlight to see if the vessel had been cracked and repaired by a filler of wax. "Without wax" is an accurate description of the integrity expected of a Christian leader. Even though we are not perfect, we do not hide our faults or sins from public view by false fillers of pretense, subterfuge, or cover-ups. Instead we follow Paul's instructions to young Timothy as he prepared him to be his successor: "Guard the good deposit that was entrusted to you—guard it with the help of the Holy Spirit" (2 Tim. 1:14). Having been called to live the holy life by God's purpose and grace (2 Tim. 1:9), we have the Holy Spirit as our sensor for sin. If we are filled with his presence, he will convict us as temptation approaches or as sin beckons. Along with this check and balance on our integrity, Paul also instructs Timothy to exercise "self-discipline" (2 Tim. 1:7). There is a difference between temptation and courtship of evil. The Holy Spirit can only be grieved if we ride roughshod over his warnings. Self-discipline is the companion of conviction brought on by the Holy Spirit.

Yet if we sin, all hope is not lost. Christian leaders must never lose the willingness to confess our sins as part of our spiritual growth. Rather than shying away from confession as a sign of weakness, Christian leaders should follow the experience of their predecessors in the faith. Those whom we extol as saints have left the testimony that the closer they came to God, the greater their sensitivity of sin and the more often they made their confession. Rather than being a sign of weakness, confession is a signal of strength. Forgiveness follows confession. Christian leaders must never assume that they no longer need to be forgiven or no longer need to ask forgiveness. It is a coin of two sides. Forgiveness is not complete until the person who is forgiven also forgives. Finally, Christian leaders must know how to say, "I am wrong. Forgive me." With these words the Christian leader puts aside power, position, and prestige and becomes the vessel "without wax" through whom the Spirit of God can work.

Henri Nouwen, in his book *In the Name of Jesus*, writes about Christian leaders demonstrating "vulnerable love" as they become accountable to the body of Christ rather than isolating themselves from its discipline.[4] While none of us can give the same challenge Jesus gave to his accusers, "Can anyone of you prove me guilty of sin?" (John 8:46), we can all strive to join the apostle Paul in his benediction, "I have fought a good fight, I have finished my course, I have kept the faith" (2 Tim. 4:7 KJV). More often than not, it all begins with a paper clip.

6

Never Swallow
Perfume

Anyone who speaks in public deals with the temptation of flattery. Those of us who speak frequently have a standard response to a public introduction that is too long and too glossy. My favorite is, "Thank you. The introduction is like fine perfume. Enjoy its fragrance, but don't swallow it."

Praise Is Intoxicating

The truth is that all of us love the fragrance of flattery and all of us are in danger of swallowing its perfume. No matter who we are, we need praise. Leaders in particular thrive on praise. Accolades come from many sides—some are earned, others are bowing to position, and still others are flattery with favors in mind. The problem comes when we begin to believe what we hear or read about ourselves. Leaders who come from humble beginnings are most susceptible to public attention and praise. If the praise is swallowed, humble people become arrogant and people with a little knowledge become "legends in their own minds."

I recall colleagues in higher education or ministry who were vaulted into celebrity status by their speaking or writing. One was a young minister who felt handicapped because he lacked an advanced degree. Sudden success came when he hit a "hot button" in the marketplace with his writing. His fee skyrocketed, his travel upgraded to first class, his messages turned into thinly-veiled advertisements for his books, and he found a way to get "Dr." added to his name. In another case, a professor took a popular relational theme and built it into a marketable system. Invitations to speak multiplied, money began to flow, and his pithy quotes brought him recognition in magazines, in newspapers, and on talk shows as a leading authority on the subject. He took these notes of praise literally. In every conversation about the subject, he cuts off all debate by forcing the issue into his diagram as the authoritative answer. When the conversation moves to other issues, he still pontificates on the subject. Even in the letters he writes to friends, he lets us know about his latest kudos and the importance of his upcoming meetings. He illustrates the hazard of swallowing the perfume of his press clippings.

Praise Is Fragile

Fame is fickle and praise is passing. Tom Wolfe is credited with the statement that in the media age, everyone can have "fifteen minutes of fame." In 1976 when *Time* magazine featured "The Year of the Evangelical," I was quoted in the article. "At last," I told myself, "you have made it to the pages of *Time* magazine." While still basking in the glory of the moment, I received a letter in the mail thanking me for speaking the Word of the Lord with the voice of a prophet. My ego leaped, and I determined to include that letter in my memoirs. The next day, however, the mail included another letter. This one came from a critic who blasted me with the words, "You are a mouthpiece for the devil." From the heights of glory, I sunk to the depths of despair.

And this was not the end of the story. Several days later I received a call from Pan American Airlines. They were checking on a ticket that I had bought from Rome to New York City. Their call completely mystified me. I had neither bought a ticket nor intended to make the flight. Further investigation showed that a Roman Catholic priest who had read the article in *Time* magazine had duped the airline into selling him a ticket using my name as credit. The story is still not over. Within this same period of days following the publication of the article, the phone rang at midnight. With a sleep-clogged voice, I answered the call only to hear a man say that he was calling from Cleveland, Ohio, and intended to commit suicide that night. Stabbed wide awake, I asked him how he got my name. He answered, "I read it in *Time* magazine." For the next hour, I tried to get him to talk about himself and his suicidal intent. He talked, but he refused to give me his phone number or home address. Finally I remembered a minister friend who lived in the Cleveland area. I told my caller about him and said I would have him make contact the next day if he would promise me that he wouldn't take his own life that night. Just as he started to give me the information, the phone went dead, and he never called back. Efforts to trace the call failed. To this day, I have no knowledge of his fate.

After this experience, I know the intoxicating power of popularity. I also know the dark side of praise. When we swallow its perfume, the reaction is sickening. Each of us needs to know how to handle praise.

Responding to Praise

Jokes take the edge off accolades that are excessive. As a rejoinder to introductions that are overdone, speakers will often say, "May God forgive you for exaggerating the facts, and may God forgive me for enjoying it." My favorite is to tell the story of an Italian farmer who was driving a little cow over a narrow bridge in northern Italy. Just as the farmer and the cow got in the middle of the bridge, a tour bus came speeding around a blind corner leading to the bridge. The bus driver, knowing that the span was too narrow for the bus, the farmer, and his cow, blew a blast on his air horn. The deafening sound so frightened the little cow that it leaped over the railing and drowned in the torrid waters below. When the bus driver rushed up to the farmer, he found him leaning over the railing, staring down at the water, and muttering over and over again, "Too bigga da honk for so smalla da cow." Jokes like this help put praise into perspective.

Downplaying excessive praise is another way of responding. Margaret Mead, perhaps our best known anthropologist of the twentieth century, had a unique response when she was presented with a $25,000 award and special gift by the board of directors of the Pacific Science Center in Seattle, Washington. After thanking us for the cash award, she turned to the silver-wrapped gift that we had given her. As she pulled at the paper, she stopped to ask, "Did you know that the final question asked of graduating students from the British School of Diplomacy is, 'How do you say thanks for a gift that you really don't want?'" Just then, the wrapping fell off a solid silver replica of the Seattle Space Needle. "Oh my," she gasped. "This certainly isn't one of them."

Frank Laubach gives us another response. When presented with an international award for his work in world literacy, he whispered, "Thank you. I must always remember that when I stand before my Lord, he will not ask to see my trophies, but he will ask to see my scars." Only a person whose life exudes the very presence of God can make that statement without insulting the host.

Jesus' Response to Praise

How does Jesus respond to praise in the Scripture record? First, we recognize that Jesus needs and relishes the praise given to him by his Father. Even before Jesus begins his public ministry, the Father responds to his baptism by announcing to the world, "This is my beloved Son, in whom I am well-pleased" (Matt. 3:17 KJV). God the Father knows that praise is an instrument that builds character and shapes destiny. As a psychologist, I have often told parents in seminars, "Love, praise, and consistency are the building blocks of a moral character and a mature person." We identify with our children on the same basis. Praise is far more effective in creating character and influencing behavior than punishment. Just as Jesus needed the praise of the Father, we need the praise of those to whom we are responsible as well as of those who look to us for leadership. The fragrance shapes us, but swallowing drowns us.

The Gospels also show that Jesus faced the downside of praise. When a young man tries to flatter him with the question, "Teacher, what good thing must I do to get eternal life?" Jesus cuts him off short. "Why do you ask me about what is good?" Going on, he says, "There is only One who is good. If you want to enter life, obey the commandments" (Matt. 19:16–17). He has similar words for the spies who are sent from the Pharisees in order to trap him. They too try flattery by addressing him, "Teacher, we know that you speak and teach what is right, and that you do not show partiality but teach the way of God in accordance with the truth. Is it right for us to pay taxes to Caesar or not?" Scripture tells us that Jesus sees through their "duplicity" and so confounds them with his answer that they are stunned into silence (Luke 20:20–26).

Even greater insight into the character of Jesus comes from the three times when we are told that he spends all night in prayer. Undoubtedly he kept many other night watches, but only three are recorded. Taken together, they become their own curriculum in leadership development. The first recorded occasion is the night before Jesus chooses his twelve disciples; the second is the night after the masses clamor to make him King; and the third is the night in the Garden of Gethsemane before his arrest and crucifixion. Each of the events that prompted a night of prayer represented a turning point in Jesus' leadership. We can understand the need for prayer before the crisis of the cross, but we may miss the importance of prayer for his staff selection and, especially, the deliverance from the temptation to be made a king! That Jesus had to flee from the flattery of the clamoring crowds into the wilderness to refocus his ministry tells us how human Jesus is and how much he is like us.

Let's admit it: We all need praise, we all want to be popular, and we all are tempted by positions of power. Because leaders thrive on praise, we are particularly vulnerable. Jesus teaches us how to respond. One, if the praise is from God, we should humbly accept it and grow with it. Two, if the praise is an attempt to get us to compromise our message, we should reject it. Three, if the praise is an attempt to trap us, we should repudiate it. Four, if the praise detracts us from our mission, we need to run from it, go to prayer, and refocus our mission.

The advice is sound. Enjoy the fragrance of praise, but don't swallow it. The effects can be fatal.

7

Never Build
without a Balcony

Leaders live in the trenches where controversial issues are confronted, contentious people are encountered, and disputable decisions are made. Without some provision for release from the pressure in order to regain perspective, leaders flame out, flunk out, and fall out. This is especially true in private or public sessions where a confrontational climate breeds reaction and hinders resolution.

Temper in the Trenches

Every executive knows what it means to have someone charge into the office with a negative agenda and an emotional chip on the shoulder. I remember most vividly the father of a student body officer who flew up the West Coast to challenge my decision dismissing his son for pushing drugs. He burst past my secretary and into the office with the threat of a lawsuit. Before I could say anything, he followed with a rapid-fire recitation of his credentials as a lawyer, a father, a civic leader, and a church member. My Scotch-Irish ancestry rose up with the thought of throwing him out of the office. Instead, I ordered him to sit down and stop his ranting. Still blustering, he obeyed, and I let my reactions take over. First I reminded him that he was in the president's office and no one talked to me like that. Next I bluntly told him that my decision was firm and if he wanted to sue me, he was welcome. Then I asked him to leave because any further conversation would take place between our attorneys. As you would guess, I threw gasoline on the fire of his rage. He started all over again and added a personalized attack on my competence. Finally I got hold of my own emotions, got up from my desk, walked over to a chair directly facing him, and spoke with a tone of reconciliation, "Wait. You say that you are a good father and a prominent church member. I too make those claims. Why don't we start on common ground?" Something happened from either my action or my words. He settled back into his chair, took on the calmness of his legal demeanor, and began to apologize for his abrupt entry and his threatening words. We were then able to go on from there to discuss my decision and explore the options for resolution without legal action.

A Trip to the Balcony

Looking back upon that encounter, I realize now that my decision to leave the authority symbol of my desk, walk over to a chair that was a companion to the one in which he sat, and face him without any barriers between us changed the dynamics of our encounter. Later I would read William Ury's book *Getting Past No: Negotiating with Difficult People*, and learn that I had unknowingly followed his advice and "gone to the balcony" by my decision to change my seat.[1] Walking around the desk and across the office and sitting in a companion chair was like leaving the stage of action and going up into the balcony to see the unfolding drama from a new perspective. My decision to move gave me the time, space, and perspective to breathe, quench the fire, and gain a measure of objectivity. From then on I never held a session in the president's office, whether friendly or hostile, without going around the desk and sitting in a chair that was purposely positioned to symbolize the common ground between us. Nor did I ever forget the lesson of creating time and space in order to gain a measure of objectivity as the alternative to reaction.

Ury says that every leader needs a balcony as a temporary retreat from the trenches in order to regain the perspective of wisdom and wholeness upon which good decisions are built. Ury's chapter entitled "Go to the Balcony" is based upon the premise that the give and take of human relationships follows a law of physics: "Action provokes reaction, reaction provokes counterreaction, and on it goes in an endless argument."[2] Going to the balcony is part of a five-step process for negotiation recommended by Ury. When confronted by a person who is making angry and unrealistic demands, Ury says, we face five challenges. First, we must control our own behavior by *refusing to react*. Second, we must *defuse the negative emotions* of our opponent and disarm him. Third, we must *change the game* by finding ways to explore the interests of both parties. Fourth, we need to help our opponent save face and *make it easy to say yes*. Fifth, we need to exercise our negotiating strength and *make it hard for the opponent to say no*.[3] Going to the balcony is central to this process, especially when we must change the name of the game in order to explore options. Ury offers three techniques for going to the balcony: We can pause and say nothing, play back the conversation, or take a time out.[4] In each case, the leader saves himself from the fatal error of making a reactive decision on the spot.

Learning the Techniques

I chuckle when I think of Ury's techniques for going to the balcony. During my brief stint as a professor at Ohio State University, I worked for a full year on a plan and budget for establishing the Center for the Study of Higher Education. Finally, in the spring, an appointment was scheduled with the dean of the School of Education and Psychology in order to present my proposal. A handsome man with an aura of authority greeted me by name and then proceeded to light his ever-present pipe while I waited. Once the sweet smell of rum-flavored tobacco filled the air, he invited me to present my proposal. It was a proud moment. The summation of a year's work went into a thirty-minute presentation for a center through which the university would develop a national identity in the field of higher education, offer a doctorate in the discipline, and serve the needs of both public and private colleges and universities. The dean listened intently, but without comment. After I finished, I waited for his response. Rather than speaking, the dean leaned back into his chair, drew deeply on his pipe, and cast a reflective look into the distance. One puff led to another as the seconds plodded past. Then he gave the signal. With practiced precision, he curled his tongue, and perfect smoke rings rose to the ceiling. "David," he said, "your presentation is most impressive. But you must be ready to give your life for it. The university is in a budget crisis and the legislature has just declared a moratorium on all new programs."

The meaning of the smoke rings became obvious. Rather than immediately responding to my proposal with a rejection, the dean "went to the balcony" in order to reflect upon his answer and let me down as easily as possible. Later I found out that this technique served as his trademark. Whenever he had to deal with controversial issues or make hard decisions, the faculty knew that they would see smoke rings before they got their answer.

As a very young college president, I got another lesson on Ury's idea. This time I saw what he meant by negotiating out of self-interest. A representative for an educational labor union met with a group of public and private college presidents in Detroit, Michigan. His assignment was to help us understand how to negotiate with union-minded teachers on our faculties. Rather than starting off with some rules of bargaining, he shocked us by saying, "College presidents have no business trying to negotiate a labor contract. You are too honest to lie, too nice to show anger, too polite to swear, and too polite to storm out of the room." For him, labor negotiations require a ruthless character with intimidating techniques that are offensive to such gentle souls as college presidents. But then he emphasized the technique for getting up and walking out of the room. By putting space and time between the negotiators, a measure of objectivity is achieved and, when the meeting reconvenes, both parties may regain their perspective.

Although we hated to admit it, we college presidents know that the labor negotiator is right. Because we are products of an academic community that depends upon good faith, sound reason, and collegiality to settle our disputes, we are not prepared for the adversarial climate created by the demands for a labor contract. Still, a lesson is learned. When I later read Ury's idea about "going to the balcony" as a way of gaining perspective during controversy, I remembered the negotiator's recommendation about leaving the room. It can be done without cursing and storming, but if done with graceful timing, it is an invaluable tool for the effective leader. Ury, of course, is talking specifically about negotiations in the business world, but I find that his premise applies to Christian relationships as well. Every leader needs to build a balcony and know when to go there.

Leading from Perspective

To be skilled in the techniques for going to the balcony during negotiations is one thing. To make the view from the balcony a perspective for all of life is quite another. In Scripture we learn how Jesus uses mountains as his balcony. On several occasions we see him leave the desert flats or the fertile valleys and climb a mountain to regain his perspective. When such moments stand out in Scripture, the meaning is intentional. Whenever Jesus speaks from the perspective of a mountain, we should pay attention.

A perspective for principle. Early in his ministry, Jesus chooses a mountain just north of Capernaum as the place to give a sermon announcing the revolutionary principles of the kingdom of God (Matt. 5–7). Standing on that site during a visit to Israel, I could see the reason for using a mountainside as a platform from which to speak to the masses below him. From that spot one can see the vista of the busy city of Capernaum, the vast expanse of the Sea of Galilee, the fertile valley of Kidron, and the Syrian mountains beyond. This is a setting where the "big picture" comes clear and the "long view" comes into focus.

A perspective for practice. Jesus climbs another mountain in the middle of his ministry (Matt. 17:1–13). From the top of the Mount of Transfiguration, he has a balcony view. In that splendorous moment, God the Father reaffirms his beloved Son with heavenly witnesses and divine glory in preparation for his passion. Before Jesus climbs the mountain, he speaks of his coming death in general terms. From the high peak, however, he sees the details of his suffering. It is a turning point in the Gospel of Mark. Before the transfiguration, the major theme is Jesus, the ministering servant. After the transfiguration, the whole story shifts to Jesus, the suffering servant. He knows precisely what is ahead. While his earlier prediction of death related to his rejection and condemnation by the Jewish hierarchy, he now tells his disciples about the betrayal that will "hand him over to the Gentiles, who will mock him and spit on him, flog him, and kill him" (Mark 10:33–34). But the perspective of the mountain has more to offer than gory truth. As God affirmed his Son in the wilderness at the start of his servant ministry, God now glorifies his Son in preparation for the suffering ministry. Going to the balcony is often a turning point in which we grasp the reality of the scene below and also see the glory of the greater good.

A perspective of progress. Toward the end of his ministry, Jesus walks the long, dry, and treacherous mountain path from Jericho to Jerusalem. Having followed that trail myself, I know the dizzy heights from which he peered out across the barren landscape. In the final steps along the twisting road is a turn that opens up a breathtaking view of the Holy City in all its glory. For Jesus, the lofty sight becomes another balcony from which he sees afar. The sight causes him to weep because he knows that his own people have rejected him and his message. "O Jerusalem, Jerusalem, you who kill the prophets and stone those sent to you, how often have I longed to gather your children together, as a hen gathers her chicks under her wings, but you were not willing" (Matt. 23:37). His plaintive cry is the word of reality that often comes from a balcony view. When we are on ground level or in the trenches, the larger picture gets distorted by details. But when we ascend to the balcony, we see both good and bad in balance. Leaders need to rise above the immediate in order to assess the status of their work and especially their progress toward their goals. In the case of Jerusalem, Jesus' cry tells us that his deepest desire was to be accepted and believed by his own people. Does he feel a sense of failure? Of course he does, on a human level. Even though he has done everything humanly possible to gather the city to himself, he will not exercise divine authority to override their freedom of choice.

The Lesson Comes Home

During the trying days of financial crisis at Seattle Pacific College (now University), mountains also served as my balcony. Growing up in Michigan, I was surrounded by flat land and stretching fields. Each summer, however, our family traveled to Massachusetts to visit relatives. Even as a child, I felt excitement every year when we began to climb the Taconic Trail east of Albany, New York. Mountains rose before us, hairpin turns awaited us, and white church spires looked like exclamation marks in the valley below. Years later, when I assumed the presidency at Seattle Pacific College, I began an instant love affair with the view of the mountains that surround the city. At one time I made the observation that when God created the world, he made the beauty of the mountains of New England and then skipped across the continent to repeat his handiwork in the Northwest. Even during the gray, wet, and dreary days of February, I would drive home from downtown over the top of Queen Anne Hill just to see the break in the clouds that revealed the craggy, snow-packed peaks of the Olympic Mountains. One look and I would recite the first verse of what became known in our family as "the McKenna Psalm": "I lift up my eyes to the hills—where does my help come from? My help comes from the LORD, the Maker of heaven and earth" (Ps. 121:1–2). I deliberately chose a path along the shores of Puget Sound for my daily jog during the years of my presidency. Running toward the south, I could see Mount Rainier on a clear day. Turning and running to the north, the craggy peaks of the Olympics almost always poked their heads through the clouds. Now, in retirement, I still go out of the way to drive over the roads that open up the vistas of distant mountains that rise east and west of our beloved city.

My unscientific conclusion is that the mountainous terrain of the Northwest accounts for the rugged pioneering spirit for which the region is known. Although stubborn individualism and religious rebellion are negative qualities of the Northwest character, the creative energy and entrepreneurial spirit are unmatched positives. Two hundred years after Meriwether Lewis and William Clark, Bill Gates and Paul Allen share that spirit. In 1969, just after we moved to Seattle, Boeing lost the contract to build the supersonic transport (SST). The infamous billboard greeted us as we drove in from the airport, "Will the last one to leave Seattle please put out the lights?" Because Seattle was known as a "company town" dependent upon Boeing, someone assumed that the SST contract represented its lifeblood. Not so, according to the facts of history. Engineers who lost their jobs at Boeing stayed in Seattle and became entrepreneurs in new ventures. A decade later, Seattle led the new economy into the field of computers, microchips, and software. Add another decade and Seattle became home for the dot-com revolution. Even though hundreds of these startup companies failed, no one can count out the innovations that are yet ahead. When you live in a world where you cannot get trapped in a concrete jungle without a view of distant mountains, the vision is always long range. As going to the balcony gives us perspective in difficult negotiations, looking up to the mountains frames the big picture for all of life.

A Mountainous Decision

As sentimental as it may seem, my love for the mountains influenced a major administrative decision one day. In 1976, when Seattle Pacific College became a University, we were searching for a dean for the new school of business. A national search led us to a man from the East Coast with credentials that clearly outdistanced other candidates. After flying him to the campus, we spent two days conducting intensive interviews. By and large, the conversations matched his credentials. His academic and professional experience in the field of business impressed the search committee, faculty, and business leaders from the community who interviewed him. As I drove him back to the airport, I indicated that I would be collecting the results of the interviews, reviewing them, and getting back to him within the week. I purposely chose the Alaskan Viaduct as our road to the airport. Skirting the edge of Puget Sound, you can look across the water and see the Olympic Mountains beyond. It turned out be one of the glorious days of the Seattle winter. A high pressure area cleared the air and added a special glint of sun on the distant mountains. With exuberance I remarked to my passenger, "Look at those mountains. Aren't they glorious?" With just a sideward glance, the candidate turned and muttered, "Mountains. To see one is to see them all." I couldn't believe what I had heard. Was our guest from the East Coast so blighted by flatlands and polluted sea that he could not see the beauty of our Northwest world? Right or wrong, I made an instant decision. The man would never be the dean of our school of business. Anyone who couldn't appreciate the view of the mountains had to have the perspective of a bean counter under a green eyeshade. After leaving him at the airport, I returned home to review the interview reports. Hidden in the comments, I saw confirming evidence that he was a strong tactician but not a strategic thinker or seer. Despite his credentials, he did not have the vision needed to launch our new school. The next day I called him to say that we had chosen not to invite him to the position. Rash judgment? Perhaps so, but when I met him again ten years later, he held a position as a professor in another school of business and felt quite content to be teaching the techniques of his field. If he couldn't see the mountains, how could he cast a vision for the future from the heights of a balcony?

I wish that I could present myself as a paragon of patience who always goes to the balcony to gain perspective on controversial issues. I can't. Just after writing this chapter, I found myself stuck in the trenches of conflict once again. In this case, incompetence aggravated by arrogance exhausted my patience. So I committed what I call "Execution by Email." In the middle of the night, I wrote an angry letter of protest and clicked "Send" without hesitation. The next morning, I reread the letter and realized that I had been so harsh that I had alienated the recipient and compounded the problem. If only I had gone to the balcony by going to bed after writing the letter, sleeping on my anger and revising the letter after regaining my perspective. It is a classic case of "Fire, ready, aim," and I am ashamed of myself.

Because I did not go to the balcony, I will have to swallow my pride and send an apology.

Oh, how slowly I learn. When I was in the presidency, I adopted a rule that I would never send negative notes to colleagues and commit "Murder by Memo." If I had a problem with a person, I always asked for a face-to-face meeting. Now I have to apply this lesson to the rapid-fire system of email. Never again will I click the "Send" button on an angry letter without first going to the balcony. Chances are that the letter will never be sent or, at least, I will ask for a personal conference.

8

Never Waste
an Interruption

I am a compulsive doodler. Now that the word *doodle* has found its way into the dictionary, it means "to scribble aimlessly, especially while preoccupied." That's me. Colleagues can always tell when I become bored with long and aimless meetings. I begin to doodle.

Glancing over my shoulder or looking across the table at my scribbles, they laugh because I am always drawing arrows rather than circles. One of them likens my doodles to a Rorschach test for leadership. The arrows, he says, symbolize my focused drive toward targeted goals. How right he is. I cannot even jog around an oval track. I have to be going someplace.

Compulsion and Closure

As proof of my straight line drive toward targeted goals, I begin every day with a list of tasks to be completed along with priorities for action. Because of an equally compulsive drive for closure, I gauge my satisfaction at the end of the day by the tasks done and the priorities met.

The only problem is that effective leadership does not work this way. Like the best-laid plans of mice and men, the daily schedule of an executive invariably includes surprises that wreak havoc with any prearranged agenda. Theoretically, I believe in "management by exception," but practically, I resent any deviations that keep me from my established goals. Interruptions, in particular, frustrate me. Whether it is an out-of-town visitor who stops in to say "hello," a peer who wants to chat for a moment, or a subordinate who needs support for a decision, I tend to receive them with a formal air, listen to them with a professional ear, and usher them out as soon as possible. Abraham Lincoln is my model. He had the front legs of the chair in the Oval Office cut one inch shorter than the back so that his guests would always feel as if they were on the way out.

All of this began to change one day while reading Henri Nouwen's book *Reaching Out*.[1] Nouwen confesses that when he was a professor of philosophy at the University of Chicago, he was so engrossed in his research and writing that he resented students who dropped in without an appointment. One day, however, he stopped to reflect on what happened during those meetings. With a flash of insight, he suddenly realized that he had his most meaningful encounters with students during those unscheduled times. After further reflection, Nouwen drew the conclusion that the students did not interrupt his business, they were his business!

The Lesson Comes to Life

While on a fund-raising trip to Columbus, Georgia, Nouwen's lesson came to life for me. I called upon William Turner, chairman of the board of the Bradley-Turner Company, an international, mega-million-dollar enterprise. Among Bill Turner's other corporate, church, and civic obligations, he served as a director of the Coca-Cola Corporation. While waiting for him in his office, I glanced at his bookshelves. One bookcase was filled with the pictures of his wife, children, and grandchildren. I had heard that Bill was best known in church on Sunday for sitting with his family and then being seen in the foyer with a grandchild in his arms. The pictures confirmed that image. Another bookcase contained picture after picture of the faces of young people ranging in age from junior high to high school and posing in informal, class-like groups or smiling like graduates for a senior picture. While I was engrossed in the pictures, Mr. Turner's executive assistant walked in to tell me that he would be delayed a few minutes. Acknowledging the delay with a nod of my head, I asked, "Who are the young people in these pictures?" Picture by picture, she began to point out the history of high school Sunday school classes that Bill Turner had taught at the United Methodist Church for years and those young people whose lives had been turned around under his faithful ministry. She introduced them to me as Mr. Turner's "other family." Just as he kept photos of his own children and grandchildren, he kept before his eyes a visual reminder of those whom he had taught and followed after they had graduated from his class. Then the executive assistant to the chairman of the board made a statement that will live forever in my mind. Without the slightest hint of apology, she said, "Mr. Turner is late because one of his Sunday school students dropped in to see him. He has a standing rule that if one of his kids comes in, I am to interrupt whatever he is doing and let the youngster come in."

Bill Turner and Henri Nouwen teach us the same truth. Interruptions are not only our business, they are our ministry. I can only imagine the heads of multinational corporations, university presidents, government officials, and civic leaders who cooled their heels in Bill Turner's office while he counseled and prayed with a teenager in trouble.

My visit to Bill Turner's office changed my style of operations as a president in higher education. Thinking about the visit on the way home, I reworked my priorities to put students first on my agenda. In fact, when I got home, I informed my executive assistant that if a student dropped by the office and wanted to see me, he or she was to have priority on my schedule. I also decided to open my office door to the hallway for an hour every day after chapel as an open invitation for students, faculty, and visitors to stop in and chat for a moment or two. By making interruptions my business, I connected with students, faculty, and visitors who would never have seen my office or chatted casually with the president. Most of all, I countered the image I had conveyed of a man so busy that no one wanted to interrupt me. As one student wryly observed, "Your openness almost makes you human."

Jesus' Ministry of Interruptions

Further curiosity led me to take a look at the Gospel of Mark in order to see how interruptions defined the ministry of Jesus Christ. I was surprised to read that Mark records more interruptions than planned events in Jesus' ministry. Time and time again, people who are sick, demon-possessed, or dead are thrust upon Jesus for healing right in the middle of his teaching. If you come right down to it, the most beautiful stories in Jesus' ministry begin as an interruption:

- the leper who stops him on the road (Mark 1:40–45)
- the paralytic who is let down through the roof (Mark 2:1–12)
- the man with the shriveled hand (Mark 3:1–6)
- the demon-possessed man of the tombs (Mark 5:1–20)
- Jairus, the ruler of the synagogue, whose daughter is dying (Mark 5:21–24 and 35–43)
- the woman with the chronic blood disease who touches Jesus' clothes (Mark 5:25–34)

- the Syrophoenician mother whose daughter has an evil spirit (Mark 7:24–30)
- the blind man of Bethsaida (Mark 8:22–26)
- the father with the epileptic boy (Mark 9:14–29)
- the parents wanting their children to be blessed (Mark 10:13–16)
- the rich young ruler (Mark 10:17–31)
- blind Bartimaeus (Mark 10:46–52)
- the woman who violates the protocol of the feast in the home of Simon the Leper in order to anoint Jesus (Mark 14:1–11)

Who can doubt? Interruptions not only define the ministry of Jesus, they are his ministry!

The Critical Interruption

In my book *Power to Follow, Grace to Lead*, I borrow the term "critical incident" from Robert Flanagan as cited in the book *People in Organizations* by Mitchell and Larson.[2] A "critical incident" is a defining moment for the character of leadership. A comic once described flying in a supersonic jet as "hours of boredom punctuated by moments of panic." Experienced leaders know what this means. Most of the time, our tasks are routine and sometimes even boring. Then, with an element of surprise, we are interrupted by a situation that makes us earn our salary and prove that we deserve to be called a leader. Defining moments come out of "critical incidents" when (1) an *unexpected circumstance* creates (2) a *personalized conflict* requiring (3) a *moral choice* with (4) *long-term consequences*.[3]

Jesus' encounter with the woman of disrepute who interrupts the Feast of Unleavened Bread in the home of Simon the Leper (Mark 14:1–9) clearly qualifies as a "critical incident." The story begins with *an unexpected circumstance*. As the guest of honor,

Jesus is reclining at the table of his host. Into the room bursts the woman. Without observing protocol, she rushes up to Jesus, breaks a costly alabaster jar of expensive perfume, and pours it on Jesus' head. Her rash action creates a *personal conflict* for Jesus. How will he respond to the violation of protocol in the house of his host? What will he say about a woman crashing a man's party in a patriarchal culture? Should he reprimand her for wasting expensive perfume? Most of all, will he put these issues above her redemption? His own disciples, led by Judas Iscariot, frame these questions for him by grumbling that the woman wasted money that could have been given to the poor.

Jesus must make a *moral choice.* "Leave her alone," he says. "Why are you bothering her? She has done a beautiful thing to me" (verse 6). Turning to his critics who raised the economic question, he answers, "The poor you will always have with you, and you can help them any time you want. But you will not always have me" (verse 7). Then, making his choice for her redemption, Jesus gently admonishes his dinner companions, "She did what she could. She poured perfume on my body beforehand to prepare for my burial" (verse 8). There is more. Jesus memorializes the moment with the prophetic message, "I tell you the truth, wherever the Gospel is preached throughout the world, what she has done will also be told, in memory of her" (verse 9).

His decision is not without *long-term consequences.* Judas Iscariot is so disillusioned by what he hears that he leaves the room and goes straight to the chief priests with the offer of betrayal (Mark 14:10–11). Of course, they are delighted to concoct a conspiracy. Judas will watch for the opportunity to hand Jesus over to them. Out of this "critical incident," the moral choice of Jesus becomes the prelude to his death.

A Career of Critical Interruptions

Interruptions never come at convenient times. As I retrace my career in presidential positions, I see an interruption at the intersection of each transition. My second presidency, for instance, took my family across the nation from Spring Arbor, Michigan, to Seattle, Washington. We had four children, aged 17, 15, 9, and just five weeks old. With the move, we pulled up a lifetime of roots with parents, family, and friends. Arriving in Seattle on July 2 with the temperature in the 90s, we camped out in the president's home at Seattle Pacific College to await our furniture and the completion of remodeling. Although I was only 39, I had learned to take transition time for the family to adjust to the move. According to my agreement with the board of trustees, I had a full month before stepping into the president's office and taking charge on August 1. All went well until July 23. I was at home unpacking boxes when the president of the National Bank of Commerce called to interrupt my work. His voice at the other end of the line is still clear in my memory: "President McKenna, we need to meet as soon as possible. I must inform you that the college has exhausted its line of credit and no more funds can be released."

Talk about an interruption of *unexpected circumstances!* I was floored by the news. According to the financial information I had received, the institution operated on narrow margins, just short of the brink of bankruptcy. Neither the audit nor the final budget report revealed the crisis. With one unexpected phone call, my month of transition went by the boards. Leaving my wife at home with our four children, including our infant son, I moved into the president's office to assume leadership of a "do or die" financial crisis. A no-nonsense review of our status showed that we had a million dollars in payables on demand, no cash to meet the next payroll, and an exhausted line of credit. Even though I was not responsible for our past, I was now responsible for our future. The financial crisis became my *personal conflict.* What would I do? Did I misread the call of God to the presidency? Was the invitation of the board of trustees misrepresented? Could a new, young president lead the institution back to solvency? Were the faculty and constituency ready for the tough decisions ahead? I could only think of the quip of a columnist about Vietnam. He wrote, "Lyndon Johnson's war has now become Richard Nixon's war." While not placing any blame upon my predecessor, I knew the financial crisis was now "McKenna's war." Should I stay or should I go? A *moral choice* had to be made.

To resolve the question, I asked my wife to join me for breakfast at a café along the Washington ship canal. Because I am from Mars and she is from Venus, I needed the balanced wisdom of her counsel. More than that, I needed the insight of a preacher's kid who had been shuttled from parsonage to parsonage during the time when Free Methodist ministers were moved every three years. With a well-planned presentation, I laid out the options. First, I could stay and succeed. But it would not be easy and it would certainly mean the long haul. Second, I could stay and fail. It was not yet clear whether the institution could be rescued from the brink of bankruptcy. If I failed, no one would want me as president. Third, I could leave under the claim of alienated affections because I did not know the situation when I accepted the presidency.

I finished my recitation. Almost as if she had not heard my labored words, the daughter of itinerant ministry looked at me and asked, "Did God call you here?" I answered, "Yes." Instantly, she said, "Then what are we waiting for? Let's go."

With Janet's intervention, I made a decision with *long term consequences* for my leadership. Four years later the college was able to pay off the nagging current debt. Seven years later we had turned around the enrollment and balanced the budget. Nine years later we were able to poise Seattle Pacific for its future role with the status of university. For me and my wife especially, however, it meant an unswerving commitment to follow the call of God. In 1982 we heard the call of God for another transcontinental move, this time from the urban setting of Seattle Pacific University to the Appalachian village that is home for Asbury Theological Seminary. Once again, an interruption marked the turning point for my presidency.

The Interruption of a Lifetime

When I arrived at Asbury Theological Seminary, I inherited a visionary program named the E. Stanley Jones School of World Mission and Evangelism. The idea was great, but the resources were limited. A professional fund-raising consultant had been retained to conduct a campaign that would fund the new program. Among the resources that had been counted on for the future was a "guesstimate" that a man named Ralph Waldo Beeson would endow Asbury in his will for approximately one million dollars. Without any evidence to back up this estimate, a one million dollar gift was included in the category of funds pledged and credited as part of the consultant's percentage fee. My first task as the new president was to define reality and fire the consultant, even under threat of suit. For the next seven years, my wife and I cultivated the contact with Mr. and Mrs. Ralph Beeson. Our president emeritus, J. C. McPheeters, had been the closest friend of the family since the turn of the century. He introduced us to the Beesons, and, after Dr. McPheeter's death, my wife and I continued to make regular visits to their home in Birmingham, Alabama. During this time we never knew how much Asbury Theological Seminary was to receive in the Beesons' will. When Mrs. Beeson died, however, the seminary received an estate gift of two million dollars. From that time on, Mr. Beeson continued to give grants for a guest house in honor of his mother and scholarship funds for international students. He also continued to adjust his will by codicils that still left us guessing. Then, as he aged into his late 80s, he sent a letter indicating that he felt Asbury needed no more funds, so the limit in his will would be approximately $700,000. We were floored by the news because we had learned that Ralph Beeson's estate totaled more than 100 million dollars! Yet we had no recourse because he had declared his decision final. We visited him personally and even sent in an Asbury professor in whose name the Beeson family had endowed a teaching chair. All to no avail.

In the semester following this disheartening news, I took my scheduled sabbatical in order to write a book. We chose to spend the time in our future retirement home in Seattle, Washington. By agreement with the provost, who served as chief executive in my absence, I would not call him and he would not call me unless he was in an emergency situation that he could not handle. With total confidence in his leadership, I could write for hours every day of the week and still take time to play with the grandkids.

While I was at my computer one afternoon, the telephone rang and my wife answered it. She had a quizzical look on her face as she brought the telephone down to me and whispered, "It's some man who wants to talk with you about the Beeson will." Red flags went up in my mind. Because I knew that vultures were already circling over the estate of Ralph Beeson, I wanted nothing to do with a caller who had found me in Seattle and interrupted my writing time. So, expecting a crank call, I picked up the phone and growled, "This is David McKenna."

In response, the caller introduced himself with a soft voice and a bit of a Southern drawl, "This is Bill Conger. Ralph Beeson has appointed me as executor of his estate." All of my defenses checked in. Ralph Beeson had no heirs, and he had never mentioned anyone named Bill Conger. Before I could speak my skepticism, the caller continued, "I am a distant cousin of Mr. Beeson and he has asked to check on Asbury." Still thinking that I might be dealing with a crank call, I played it safe by asking, "How can I help?" Bill Conger took charge of the conversation by telling me that he was a retired U.S. Army colonel who had retired in Birmingham, Alabama, and visited with Mr. Beeson every day. He went on to say that he had never heard of Asbury, knew no one on the campus, and had decided to start his investigation with the president. My defenses dropped a little, but I decided that I had to check out the caller before becoming more involved. So, I went into a delaying tactic, asking Mr. Conger if we could arrange a meeting on the campus so that we could meet personally and talk about the seminary. He said, "Yes, I can drive up anytime. Let me know when we can meet."

As soon as he hung up, I called the vice president of advancement on campus and asked him to go to Birmingham immediately to check out the name Bill Conger. He left immediately, did the check, and called me to say that Colonel Conger was indeed the newly appointed executor of the Ralph Beeson estate. Meanwhile, Bill Conger was doing his own double-checking on Asbury. He called upon a United Methodist pastor and asked him about the seminary. The pastor answered, "I have never been to Asbury. I know none of the professors. But I do know one thing about the graduates. *They can preach!*"

Colonel and Mrs. Conger visited the campus several times, absorbed our history, read our books, and spent hours talking with our faculty. Asbury's reputation for preaching became the cornerstone of Conger's interest. Complementing this commitment, his wife, Betty, was the daughter of a great United Methodist preacher. She knew firsthand the power of the pulpit.

The rest of the story is a miracle of grace. We had despaired over Mr. Beeson's conclusion that Asbury needed no more than $700,000 for scholarships in his will. But each time that Colonel Conger came to the campus, he stepped up the amount. The $700,000 became 1.2 million, 1.2 million became 9 million; 9 million became 21 million; and 21 million became 41 million, all in the first distribution from the estate. When all of the gifts were totaled, Asbury Theological Seminary invested 21 million dollars in complete campus renewal, created a high-tech infrastructure for serving a world parish, and endowed chairs for a world-class faculty. Most important of all, the endowment was increased from 7 million dollars to more than 120 million dollars, fourth largest among all graduate schools of theology and first among free-standing seminaries. Asbury was literally launched into the ministry of international leadership because of Bill Conger's interest in a place that produced graduates who could preach.

I still break out in a cold sweat when I think back to the unexpected telephone call from a total stranger who interrupted my sabbatical. What if I had followed my first inclination and rejected the call or cut short the caller? Like Henri Nouwen, I learned the lesson of leadership, "Interruptions are my business."

9

Never Die
from Failure

Harry Truman is credited with the jab at timid leaders, "If you can't stand the heat, get out of the kitchen." He might well have added the corollary quote, "If you can't handle failure, get out of leadership."

Usually when we think about great leaders, we begin by noting their successes. But if you ask them personally to assess their leadership, they will tell you about the way in which they handled difficult situations and learned from failure. Going a step farther, they will remember that they learned more from their failures than from their successes. To quote Harry Truman again, when asked what he did when he made a "bum decision," he answered, "I just go out and make another one."[1] Winston Churchill, Truman's companion in world leadership, is legendary for his momentous failures as well as his magnificent achievements. Reviewing his own life, he once quipped, "Success is going from failure to failure without losing your enthusiasm."[2]

The question, then, is not whether leaders will make mistakes or fail, but how they will handle these situations. Three realities guide us.

To Lead Is to Risk

Risk is synonymous with leadership. Anyone who is adverse to risk will never be able to lead. Whether you read the story of movements that have changed the course of history or the autobiographies of those who have led those movements, they have one thing in common: risk-taking. Skip through human history and identify the leaders of destiny. You can find some of them in the book entitled *Great Leaders, Great Tyrants?* by Arnold Blomberg.[3] Because they are risk-takers, they are often perceived as tyrants. Familiar names come forward as we read about the apostle Paul, Augustine, Calvin, Beckett, Wesley, Luther, Tyndale, Kierkegaard, Gandhi, Churchill, Bismarck, Cromwell, DeGaulle, Mao Zedong, Queen Elizabeth, Sir Walter Raleigh. On and on the list goes. As human leaders, they all have feet of clay. Their greatness, whether as leaders or tyrants, arises from the fact that they took risks to state their case, take their stand, and change the world.

Advancing from the past into current history, we learn that survivors in the corporate world are those companies that have put their money into R and D—usually identified as Research and Development, but perhaps just as well described as "Risk and Daring." Bill Gates, for instance, takes the model of risk for Microsoft from the Boeing Company. He says that Boeing bets the company on breakthrough aviation products in every other decade. In the 1950s, Boeing gambled on the first all-jet 707 passenger plane; in 1968 on the 747, the first jumbo jet; and in the 1990s on the 777, the first digitally designed airplane. Now, in Seattle, we are hearing about the twenty-first century gamble on the 7E7 sub-sonic cruiser as a challenge to its Airbus competitor. Using the Boeing example, Gates says, "To win big, sometimes you have take big risks."[4]

On a more personal note, I recall a mentoring session with Ross Mooney, author of the "Mooney Problem Checklist," when I was a fledgling professor at Ohio State University. To explain to me his theory of human development, Ross stood with both feet together and balanced on the floor. "This is the stance of stability or equilibrium," he said. "To remain in this position, however, assures no forward movement, and, if you stand long enough, you will fall." Ross then put one foot forward, saying, "Now I am out of balance and under tension. I cannot remain in this position forever without succumbing to the stress. The natural inclination is to bring the back foot forward so that the body is back into balance. By repeating this process again and again—*balance, imbalance, balance*—the whole body moves forward in a walk or a run." Mooney described this process as "mobile equilibrium" or balance in motion. He then emphasized his point by saying, "There is no forward movement without the risk of stepping into imbalance." In the same breath, he added the fact, "Leaders must know when to take the step of risk and when to pause while the organization gets its balance."

Because I see myself as a risk-taker, Mooney's lesson has stayed with me. A few months prior to our conversation, I had left the security of the position as vice president at Spring Arbor Junior College, my alma mater and hometown for my wife, in order to test the uncharted waters of a professorship at Ohio State University. The move represented a giant step into imbalance for me, my wife, and our young family. Because Janet was a preacher's kid whose childhood and teenage years had been marked by frequent moves from parish to parish, she took the risk in stride and provided the family with its stability. A year and a half later, after my program was put on hold, I took a more secure step back to a faculty position at the University of Michigan. Even before settling into that role, however, the invitation came to assume the presidency of Spring Arbor Junior College with the assignment to build a four-year, accredited liberal arts college. Colleagues in higher education could not understand my decision to accept the presidency. One professorial friend likened the decision to "riding off into the sunset" as far as my future leadership in higher education was concerned. Nevertheless, we met our goal for developing a four-year college within a seven-year term, and I was ready for another step forward.

This time the call came from Seattle Pacific College, over half a continent away and close to the hub of a booming metropolis. Once again leaving the security of family, position, and our home state, my family and I followed the trail of Lewis and Clark to the Northwest. More than distance made the move a risk. Midwestern and Northwestern cultures are worlds apart. It took fourteen years to achieve the goal of developing university status for the school. But once I was secure in the position, the invitation to the presidency came from Asbury Theological Seminary.

Having adjusted to the urban culture of Seattle and the pioneer mentality of its people, our family found ourselves going back to the village culture of Wilmore, Kentucky, and the traditional Southern mentality of its people. Add to this change in cultures the challenge of a shift in leadership from a university to a graduate school of theology. Another giant step put me back into tipsy imbalance. Yet through these experiences, I discovered that Ross Mooney was right. Mobile equilibrium is a good way to describe my career in higher education. By taking the risk of imbalance, I moved forward a step at a time. Looking back, I can see the footprints of balance, imbalance, and balance once again. The journey is one for which I have no regrets.

To Risk Is to Fail

A leader who takes risks will experience failure. With tongue in cheek, I have often talked about the "white elephants" that every college or university president leaves behind. In my first presidency, I was enamored with white pillars on brick buildings.

One day at lunch, I sketched the small, nondescript administration building on campus and added a portico with white, fluted pillars as the next project in the presidency. For years this semi-Grecian building served as the center of the campus. Now those white pillars typify the mongrel days of campus architecture when buildings were constructed at lowest cost without a unifying style or design. Each time I return to the campus, I look at those pillars and pray that the alumni will not remember them as "McKenna's white elephant."

College and university presidents are also victims of fads that become failures. In the decade of the 1960s, for instance, futurism was in vogue. Higher education responded by spending millions of dollars on ten-year plans for institutional development. Slick brochures outlining projections such as enrollment growth, student quality, curricular expansion, campus construction, faculty scholarship, and national stature became common pieces of literature for raising funds, influencing constituencies, and impressing parents of prospective students. These same plans fell victim to the social turmoil of the late 1960s and early 1970s when the campus became the center of protest and violence. Long before the ten-year cycle of planning was complete, the glossy projections had become an embarrassment to their makers. We educators learned what a critic of futurism means when he advises, "If you must plan, plan often."

Great leaders who take risks know the reality of failure. In his book *Leading Minds: An Anatomy of Leadership,* Howard Gardner tells the stories of eleven individuals who are identified as "great" in the domain where they served: Margaret Mead, J. Robert Oppenheimer, Robert Maynard Hutchins, Alfred P. Sloan, George C. Marshall, Pope John XXIII, Eleanor Roosevelt, Martin Luther King Jr., Margaret Thatcher, Jean Monnet, and Mahatma Gandhi.[5] While Gardner seeks to find characteristics of greatness in these leaders, he does not spare the facts regarding their failures. They may have failed because of changing conditions, unexpected historical upheavals, overly exclusionary or inclusionary stories, excessive demands by others, or excessive demands upon themselves.[6] This occurred so often that Gardner concludes, "in one way or another, all experienced failure: thwarting their mission, loss of their position, or both."[7] In the short run, these leaders may have appeared to be ineffective, but in the long run, they have a claim to greatness because they set in motion a series of events with significant, long-term consequences. In the appendix of the book, Gardner balances the ultimate successes of the eleven leaders with their failures.[8] The claim to greatness is not unbridled success in the short run, but significant change over a period of time.

To Fail Is to Learn

Gardner's study of greatness in *Leading Minds* confirms the observation of Bennis and Nanus in their book *Leaders* when they write, "Perhaps the most impressive and memorable quality of the leaders we studied was the way they responded to failure."[9] One of their subjects summed up this response by saying, "If I have an art form of leadership, it is to make as many mistakes as quickly as I can in order to learn."[10] Another said, "It's like learning to ski. If you're not falling down, you're not learning."[11] Of course, such an outlook requires a good dose of self-esteem, which ultimately translates into a leader's ability for self-deployment in order to empower others.

Bill Gates, in his book *Business @ the Speed of Thought*, dispels any notion that Microsoft is successful in every venture it undertakes. He introduces the chapter entitled "Convert Bad News to Good" by writing, "Once you embrace unpleasant news not as a negative but as evidence of a need for change, you aren't defeated by it. You're learning from it. It's all in how you approach failures. And believe me, we know a lot about failures at Microsoft."[12] Gates follows up this introduction by citing the major failures of the Multiplan spreadsheet, a database called Omega, the personal digital assistant, the Microsoft at Work project, and the TV-style Internet shows on MSN. He then confesses, "The weight of all of our failures could make me too depressed to come in to work. Instead I am excited about the challenges and by how we can use today's bad news to help solve tomorrow's problems."[13]

So, as Bennis and Nanus remind us again, leaders never focus on failure. To make their point, they tell the story of Karl Wallenda, known around the world as the greatest high-wire artist of all time. Throughout his career, Wallenda dazzled audiences with his death-defying walk on a wire strung several stories above the street below. During those years, he never focused on falling but only on walking the wire. On his last walk, which led to his fatal fall, his wife noted that he spent most of his time making sure that he would not fall. Never before had this been his obsession. By fixing his attention on not falling, he was destined to fail.[14]

The "Wallenda factor" applies to all of leadership. If the focus is on failure, the fall will be inevitable. So the question is whether we take risks with the fear of failure or as an opportunity for learning. Early in my presidential career, I took on the task of a capital fund campaign for the development of the new four-year college at Spring Arbor. Without any experience in the field, we retained a professional fund-raising consultant with a national reputation. The cost was too high for our meager budget, but other presidents told me that this was the only way to go. Dreams of funding from foundations, major donors, the local community, and the church constituency unfolded as our consultant foresaw several million dollars for scholarships, construction, and day-to-day operations. For months our energies went into organizing the campaign, recruiting the leadership, researching foundation giving, and identifying major donors. The end result? We paid the consultant a high dollar and raised only a small part of our total goal. In other words, we failed. With the scars still fresh, I did a postmortem on the project, noting what went wrong and why. Foremost, I realized that we were not ready for the campaign. We were not known in the larger community, we had not introduced ourselves to foundations, campaign leadership could not be recruited, and presidential priorities for developing a new college took too much time away from contacts with major donors. I also learned that some professional fund-raisers will set rosy goals in order to get a retainer. Sadder but wiser, I never let that happen again. From then on I knew where the rocks were and walked on them to success in future campaigns.

To Learn Is to Grow

Leaders grow when they learn from risk that may include failure. In the mid-1990s, I qualified as a consultant using psychological instruments to assist executive leaders in assessing and advancing their careers. After identifying the strengths and weaknesses of the leaders through the use of the instruments, several opportunities for growth are suggested as options for the client. Key to these opportunities is the G.A.G. or "Going Against the Grain" type of experience. As the name implies, these experiences push the leader out of the comfort zone and into the arena of risk where growth takes place. Examples of G.A.G. experiences include changes in the scope, scale, level, and type of leadership responsibility. Each case brings a risk with the possibility of failure, and the greater the risk, the greater the potential for growth.

After being introduced to the G.A.G. experience, I reflected upon the spurts of growth in my own career. The move from the security of my position as vice president of Spring Arbor Junior College to assistant professor of the faculty at Ohio State University changed the scope, scale, level, and type of my responsibility. Yet during the year and a half when I was developing the Center for the Study of Higher Education, I had the opportunity to serve out of the president's office and interview every vice president and dean of a university of 30,000 students. Even though my program was shelved by a legislative moratorium, I gained a crash course in university administration.

At Spring Arbor Junior College, the G.A.G. of a startup for a new program was unforgettable. Later the move from the fledgling Spring Arbor College to well-established Seattle Pacific College became another G.A.G. experience as I changed cultures, increased the scope and scale of my leadership, inherited the responsibility for turnaround management, and built the institution to university status. Still another G.A.G. experience awaited me with the change from Seattle Pacific University to Asbury Theological Seminary. Few of the functions of leadership transferred from a university of liberal and professional studies to a graduate school of theology preparing students for ministries in the church. The call of the G.A.G experience at Asbury was for break-out leadership that would give the school international identity in the "world parish" of the Wesleyan movement. Now I see the spurts of growth I underwent in each of the risks I took.

Although the long-term consequences of these G.A.G. experiences show an aura of success, I also remember the wrenching moments when I teetered on the brink of failure. At Ohio State, the program was scuttled by the legislature. At Spring Arbor College, regional accreditation for the four-year program hung in the balance until the last minute. At Seattle Pacific University, only the long-term reputation of the school held off the creditors. And at Asbury Theological Seminary, I was caught in the middle of a rift between the board and the faculty over the development of a new school of world mission and evangelism. In each case, I walked a razor's edge.

We need not feel this is a negative note. A leader who takes a risk is always in tension between failure and learning. If the focus is on failure, the expectation will come true. But if the focus is on learning, even failure becomes an opportunity for self-discovery, new knowledge, and personal growth.

10

Never Hide behind
a Gas Mask

Leadership would be easy if our organizations were like computers. Without minds of their own, they would respond automatically to the orders we give them. Although we know that this is not the case, studies of organizational behavior often begin with a mathematical model not unlike a computer. These studies assume that our organizations are rational entities in which leaders make linear decisions. In this model, two plus two always equals four, the lines of authority are always clear, and all of the connections between the parts are obvious. If organizations were like computers, an intricate bundle of chips, cells, and connectors, leadership would be a no-brainer.

Organizations Are Flesh and Blood

The real world refutes the image of a computer as the ideal of an organization. Organizations are not rational, leadership is not linear, and relationships are not clear and clean. The image of a human organism is a far more realistic way to describe an organization. While built upon a skeletal structure, the pulsation of vital organs, the sensitivities of flesh and skin, and the permeation of blood flow create a body that is unique in itself. Leadership of an organism requires a finely tuned balance of managing facts and feelings within the body as well as its actions and reactions to changes outside the body.

Take this image one step further. When an organization is considered an organism peopled by human beings, a family appears. Having been introduced to the mathematical model of leadership in the 1960s, I proceeded to fashion my leadership according to this model. It wasn't disastrous, but it came close. After stumbling through the rational and linear decisions that characterized my earlier leadership, I was introduced to the theory of organization advanced by Edwin H. Friedman in his book *Generation to Generation: Family Process in Church and Synagogue.*[1] Far removed from the mathematical model of the past, Friedman describes an organization as a family system, with all of the interacting and elusive dynamics that this implies. Within this framework, he identifies the characteristics of what he called a "self-differentiated" leader. At the risk of oversimplifying Friedman's definition, a self-differentiated leader is one who can objectively state the case as head of the body while maintaining relationships with the members of the body. Biblical truths leap forward in these words. John describes Jesus as a person who was filled with grace and truth (John 1:14). Paul picks up the same theme in his letter to the Ephesians when he identifies maturity in Christ with the ability to "speak the truth in love" (Eph. 4:15). Friedman's insights turned my approach to leadership upside down.

Living in an Anxious Age

Friedman begins with the assumption that we are living in a "chronically anxious age." Most of us agree. But we do not fully realize the implications of this anxiety until it is brought into the workplace. Anxious individuals can poison an organization, render it dysfunctional, and contaminate its relationships. Friedman is so bold to say that he can instantly read the health of an organization by the way that leadership handles dysfunctional members who create a toxic environment with their feelings and sabotage its effectiveness with their attitudes. Paralleling this reading of leadership behavior, he also asks how "self-differentiated" people are treated in the organization. If self-differentiated people are respected and nurtured while saboteurs must either change or be dismissed, Friedman considers that a healthy organization.

Every organization, religious or secular, is vulnerable to the attacks of dysfunctional persons who bring their anxiety into the workplace. Religious organizations, particularly those that claim to be Christian, may be even more susceptible. By identifying ourselves as a "family" and calling each other "brother" and "sister," we create high expectations for our relationships. In truth, because we love each other so much, we can hurt each other more deeply.

During one of my presidencies, I hired a vice president for finance from a large, public university. As a Christian in that secular setting, both his competence and his credibility witnessed to his faith. He came to us with a call to ministry in the field of finance and with the anticipation of being part of the Christian community. After three years in the role, however, he surprised me by submitting his resignation. When pressed for a reason, he answered, "In a secular institution, administrators fight and cuss over budget decisions. Afterwards, they go out and have a beer together. Here, in the Christian institution, we pray before we meet and are always polite in our negotiations, but every decision is taken personally. I can't handle the hurt." His resignation cautioned me about being too glib in speaking about being the "body of Christ" or the "family of God." Our strength can also be our weakness.

Since that experience, I have often compared the Christian family to the Irish family of my McKenna ancestry. As an Irish family, we have our internal squabbles, but no one dares to attack us without learning how unified we can be. So I ask myself, "How in the world can you lead such a gang of divided members and unified defenders?" Friedman says that the first rule for an organizational leader in a chronically anxious age is to avoid putting on a gas mask. When the toxic fumes of division fill the air, a leader cannot hide behind the protection of a gas mask with the hope that the gases will dissipate. He or she must address the issues, confront the offenders, and make life-saving decisions for the beleaguered family.

An executive in a software company chose a gas mask to avoid the toxic protests of malcontents on his staff. He escaped an immediate crisis but transferred the poisonous environment to his successor. A dysfunctional team in a toxic environment is an unfair legacy. His successor had to clean house in order to get the team moving forward again. While a gas mask avoids confrontation, it exposes a weak leader who penalizes himself, his organization, and his successor.

Dealing with a Dysfunctional Family

No leader can escape the standing rule: *a confrontation delayed is a confrontation escalated.* I have paid the personal price for violating this rule. Hiding behind a gas mask, I wanted to believe that a dysfunctional person would either go away or be rejected by other members of the institutional family. I confess that I also wanted to avoid a direct and nasty confrontation that would test my leadership. It never works this way. In one case, months dragged into years, toxic gases spread through the family, and we were literally paralyzed by my failure to act. I continued to ignore the saboteur, and other members of the team tolerated him. Perhaps in the spirit of brotherhood and under the guise of unity in the ministry, his colleagues excused him as the victim of a dysfunctional home whom the Christian community should embrace. Finally, when confrontation could no longer be avoided, I challenged the person privately and addressed the issue in a public statement. The result was a question from members of the community whom I had thought would side with him, "Why didn't you make this decision a long time ago?" By donning a gas mask to avoid a toxic environment created by a dysfunctional member, I had forfeited my leadership, and only aggressive intervention could bring it back.

Since that time I have become a disciple of Friedman's theory of self-differentiated leadership. Self-differentiation implies a self-understanding and a sense of self-esteem by which the leader can engage the issues and the climate of the organization with a balance of objectivity and subjectivity. If one is overbalanced on objectivity, others feel a sense that the leader is isolated from the relational needs of the people. If one is overbalanced on subjectivity, the leader becomes so immersed in the relationships that the issues cannot be resolved. Counseling psychology gives us further understanding of self-differentiation by drawing the comparison between "empathy" and "sympathy." When a counselor is sympathetic with a client, objectivity is lost in feelings. Empathy, however, means communicating an understanding of the client's feelings while maintaining the objectivity required for solving the problem. In the same sense, a self-differentiated leader is empathetic in dealing with the complexity of institutional and relational issues. Friedman uses the analogy of the head to the body as an example. A leader loses self-differentiation as the head of the body if the head gets detached from the body by the loss of subjectivity or immersed into the body by loss of objectivity. A head that speaks with conviction while staying attached to the body through the connection of the neck is Friedman's image of self-differentiation.

With full credit to the Rabbi Friedman, I have recast his principles into "NO means GO" categories. A self-differentiated leader:

1. Never loses connectional relationships when making convictional decisions;
2. Never casts blame when stating the case;
3. Never puts on a gas mask in a toxic environment;
4. Never creates a triangle (involves a third party) in order to diffuse responsibility;
5. Never delays direct confrontation when needed;
6. Never hesitates in dealing with saboteurs.

These principles make a difference in my executive leadership. Not only do I exercise them with good results, but I see another of Friedman's ideas take hold. He says that he can read the health of an organization by the way in which the leader deals with self-differentiated people. Who wins in our organizations? Is it the dysfunctional saboteur who paralyzes the family? Or is it the self-differentiated person who tells the truth while maintaining the relationships of a healthy family?

Jesus, the Model of Self-Differentiated Leadership

Jesus is our example for self-differentiated leadership. John 1:14 is one of the passages of Scripture that most reveals the leadership style of Jesus. In the poignant words that we may miss by a quick reading, John describes Jesus as a leader "full of grace and truth." No terms of contemporary theory carry more weight in understanding the meaning of self-differentiated leadership than these words. Jesus spoke the convictions of truth without losing the connections of grace. Our human tendency is to fall off one side or the other.

In confrontations with dysfunctional people, for instance, we tend to temper the truth and overdo grace. It is like cutting off the dog's tail an inch at a time. A clear, surgical cut is often more redemptive than incisions made an inch at a time. Especially when dealing with saboteurs, the patience of Christian brotherhood must give way to decisive action. To take this path, however, is to walk through a minefield. We must count on the apostle Paul to show us the way when he urges the Corinthians to purge from their body those who defy the Christlike standards of faith and practice. Although he exercises all of the patience of grace for immature believers, he does not hesitate to act with surgical precision when a spiritually dysfunctional member of the family threatens its existence. "On my return I will not spare those who sinned earlier or any of the others, since you are demanding proof that Christ is speaking through me" (2 Cor. 13:2–3). Paul has the same word for the Ephesian church. Rather than continuing to tolerate the "cunning and craftiness of men in their deceitful scheming" (Eph. 4:14) who are tossing the infant church on waves of disbelief, he says, "Instead, speaking the truth in love, we will in all things grow up into him who is the Head, that is, Christ" (Eph. 4:15). Dysfunctional saboteurs who undermine the unity of the body of Christ must hear the truth with love.

The Lesson Comes Home

All of us wish that the issues we ignore would just go away. They don't. Even the little issues we ignore take on a life of their own and grow into crisis proportions. This working rule applies particularly to situations that call for a leader to confront face-to-face the person or persons who have an investment in the issue. But let's be honest: whether we are cowardly or unsure, more often than not, our usual strategy is to delay the confrontation with the hope that the issue will either go away or resolve itself.

Experience says that this does not happen. Although I consider myself neither cowardly nor unsure, I will avoid confrontation until I have no other alternative. This is wrong and costly. Without exception, my delayed confrontations fester until an institutional crisis is provoked. I recall a bright young professor whom I tapped for a key role in my administration. He passed every test except taste and judgment. His taste tended to be extravagant, and his judgment tended to be immature. Looking back, I didn't feel as if these were character flaws. Rather, I saw them as indications of a bright and bumptious person who needed guidance and discipline. I was wrong, and I failed him. Just before the conclusion of my tenure in that institution, he made some judgment calls that could no longer be ignored. Earlier questions about his taste had now escalated into decisions that were detrimental to the institution. The confrontation came too late. He defied my authority, and our relationship fell apart. I had no choice but to fire him. Reflecting back upon that nasty experience, I have no doubt that early confrontation would have solved the problem and probably saved the person.

Conflict is inevitable in any organizational family. We are wrong to assume that a conflict-free environment is the sign of organizational health. It is not. The key to organizational health is how the family handles the conflict. If the leader dons a gas mask, conflict in the family will fester, poison the climate, sabotage the unity, and spoil the legacy. By refusing to wear a gas mask, a leader is put to the supreme test. Only a self-differentiated leader can invoke the conviction of confrontation without losing connection with the body of the organization and maintaining its relationships. Obviously this kind of leadership is rare because of the degree of maturity required. Yet it is the goal to which all leaders aspire.

Expectations for Christian leaders are even higher. To speak the truth with love is impossible from a human standpoint. But with the resources of the Holy Spirit, it is a very present possibility. With his mind and his Spirit, we have no need for a gas mask. The conviction of truth can be spoken without losing the connection of love.

11

Never Sniff
at Symbols

Symbol-making is a gift of God for our humanity. Lower animals neither make symbols nor understand their meaning because they lack the gift of self-awareness. Even human generations that reject symbols of the past end up creating symbols of their own. Hippies of the 1960s aimed their protest, trashing, and bombing at the symbols of a capitalistic culture. In their place, they created a peace sign, grew a beard, held a flower, and put on sandals. Their grungy uniforms symbolized their culture as readily as white shirts, plain ties, and blue blazers symbolized IBM.

The Significance of Symbols

Any doubts about the significance of symbols disappear in light of the events of September 11, 2001. In their carefully planned plot, suicide terrorists chose the central symbols of American democracy and capitalism when they targeted the White House, the Pentagon, and the World Trade Center. Even though they missed the White House, the depth of rage from direct hits on the Pentagon and the World Trade Center prompted the President to declare war against terrorism throughout the world. No wonder that Tom Peters believes that the making and meaning of symbols is one of the most powerful tools in the hands of a leader.

Think of the biblical symbols that God uses to communicate with his creation. Beginning with the snake in the garden, graphic representations parade through Scripture—a rainbow, a burning bush, a golden calf, a wooden ark, a holy temple, and a wheel within a wheel. Then we see a guiding star, a descending dove, a thundering voice, and a blaze of glory leading us to a meal of broken bread and poured wine, a woeful garden, a crown of thorns, a cruel cross, an empty tomb, a nail-scarred hand, fiery tongues, and a rushing wind. Finally, apocalyptic events appearing in the images of seven candlesticks, a golden throne, a marriage supper, and a judgment court come to culmination in the vision of a new heaven and a new earth. Sadly, many of these symbols are being ignored by the upcoming generation of believers. Overhead screens, bandstands, theater seats, and high-amp systems carry their own symbolic value, but they are not the rich symbols of meaning for the Christian faith. As we have been informed, the current generation is the first to grow up without a prayer to remember, a Scripture verse to know, and a hymn to sing. Having robbed our children of these gifts, we compound their loss by taking away the symbols of the faith.

Symbols of Character

The power of religious symbols was impressed upon me during my graduate study in the 1950s. Researchers of that era followed Roman Catholic, Jewish, and Protestant students into their college and university careers. As I recall from memory, a large majority of the Roman Catholics continued to practice their faith, even if nominally, while a minority of the Protestants and a much smaller percentage of the Jews made the same claim. Attempting to explain these differences, the researchers concluded that the Roman Catholic students identified their faith with the symbols of the church that were meaningful to them as children—fingering the beads of the rosary, making the sign of the cross, kneeling for prayer, and seeing the iconic figures of the Christ. Confirmation added the symbols of the sacraments, the liturgy, and the rituals of Roman Catholic tradition. Protestant students did not have these memories, and even though Jewish worship may have its own symbols, they did not have the same potency in influencing children. Although the statistics of the study are dated, the outcome still influences my leadership.

Marketing experts are especially attuned to the power of symbols. Four of the most potent marketing symbols come to mind: a Coca-Cola bottle, the Golden Arches of McDonald's, the Nike "Swoosh" logo, and the hood ornament of Mercedes-Benz cars. These four symbols are recognized worldwide as distinctive trademarks for leaders in their respective fields. Every competitor is chasing them futilely because they lack a similar symbol of distinction. Avis auto rental is one of few companies to find success in competing with a worldwide leader. By admitting "We're Number Two" and trailing after Hertz, Avis has become a formidable competitor. Fast food competitors of McDonald's, however, have not been able to match the Golden Arches. At the age of two, our youngest daughter could spot the Golden Arches a block or two away and point her daddy to "Mac-Donoughs." Ask any child how they remember Wendy's, Burger King, Jack-in-the-Box, or Big Boy. Only the most precocious will have an answer. Lacking a symbol of distinction, the best these chains can do is build their franchises close enough to a McDonald's to offer an option and catch the overflow business.

Hard-nosed business leaders tend to be skeptical about symbols. They are viewed as necessary nonsense in marketing plans but hardly the stuff out of which strong executive leadership is made. Tom Peters and Robert Waterman made this assumption before writing the book *In Search of Excellence*, in which they identified 300 of the best-run companies in America.[1] To their surprise, however, they discovered that the most excellent businesses had adopted a symbol in the form of a sign or a slogan that communicates a qualitative difference between them and their competitors. Symbols that used to be considered faddish and slogans that were ridiculed as corny are now serious tools of a business plan. As an example, in the summer of 2002, Microsoft CEO Steve Ballmer took his executive team on a retreat in order to update and project forward the future of the company. Originally, Bill Gates advanced the vision of "a PC on every desktop and in every home." In 1999 that vision evolved into "empowered people through great software." Now, in the chaotic climate of technological change and the litigious climate of competitors in the courts, Ballmer and his team spent several days together before coming up with the twenty-first-century vision, "your potential, our passion." An obvious shift in the focus of Microsoft is evident in the statement. The mission has gone from the home to the world and from the functional operation of a PC to the relational connections of human potential. As idealistic as the latest slogan may seem, it does promise to reshape the company and define its direction for the future.

In my first professional development conference after becoming a college president, I encountered the full force of symbolic leadership in an unexpected setting. College and university presidents met with campus planners and architects at Harvard University. Arland Chris-Janer, a well-known architect, was one of the speakers for the plenary sessions. In approaching campus planning or building construction, he drew our attention to what he called the "front door." Whether it is the entry to the campus or a building on the campus, Chris-Janer said that the front door is a symbol that sets the tone for all that follows.

If the front door is designed to say "Welcome" and the visitor walks into "humanized space," a climate is created and a culture is communicated. Visitors expect to be cordially greeted and graciously treated. If, on the other hand, the entry is drab and impersonal, nothing of warmth or elegance inside the door can make up for the tone-setting point. His conclusion still sticks in my mind. He said, "We build our buildings, and then they build us."

To punctuate his point, Chris-Janer told about the design for the Protestant chapel at Dachau, the Nazi concentration camp. A visitor enters through a wide door that immediately narrows into a darkened hallway leading downward into the building. Proceeding through this tunnel, the visitor walks into the open sanctuary of the chapel with its pews, altar, Bible, and cross. After pausing to reflect on the horrendous evil unleashed in the concentration camp and praying "Never again," the visitor exits out the other side to walk up a rising plane back into the light of day. The symbol, of course, is the death and resurrection of Jesus Christ. After standing in front of the cremation ovens and looking up at the death-dealing shower heads, we reexperienced the Christian message through the symbols of the architecture. As Christ went from death on the cross into the depths of hell, he arose as our hope for the newness of life. The symbols speak louder and clearer than any words that could be uttered.

After the conference at Harvard, I made it a point to use the symbols of our entry points to set the tone of the campus. Open doors, warm colors, humanized space, and a smiling receptionist became standard for the buildings we built or remodeled. But not without criticism. When I transformed the entry point for visitors and student prospects at Asbury Theological Seminary from hospital-colored walls and barbershop-tiled floors to the warmth of Williamsburg blue walls and the softness of beige carpeting, I got a call accusing me of choosing the devil's colors. Does the devil love blue and beige? I don't know. One thing, however, is sure. People take their symbols seriously.

In my first presidency, I was given the assignment of advancing Spring Arbor Junior College to fully-accredited, four-year college status. Although higher education was my field of specialization and I had served on the faculty of two state universities, I needed the help of a wise and experienced head before launching the venture. Tom Jones, president of Earlham College and one of the most esteemed leaders in American higher education, agreed to consult with us. Dr. Jones visited the campus armed with a question. Everyone he met, from students to trustees, heard him ask, "What's the Big Idea?" He wanted to discover the reason for the existence of this little college. Another way of putting the question came in the provocative inquiry, "If this school did not exist, would it have to be invented?"

After collecting the responses from across the campus, Jones returned with a summary of the comments and the story of what he called "The Earlham Idea." He too had inherited a small, struggling college when he accepted the presidency at Earlham. He began by searching the history of the institution for its roots and then advanced to asking the same question about the "Big Idea" far and wide on the campus, in the community, and across the constituency. Out of that inquiry, the Earlham Idea came to life in the words, "A quality liberal arts college in the Quaker tradition." As simple as it may seem, the slogan became the guiding force for bringing the school into national prominence.

Tom Jones was using the same approach with us at Spring Arbor College. He did not answer his question for us. Rather, he challenged us to put the Spring Arbor Idea into the fewest words possible and seal it with a symbol. Out of his challenge, the Spring Arbor concept was born: *"a community of learners engaged in the serious study of the Christian liberal arts, totally committed to Jesus Christ as the perspective for learning, and engaged as critical participants in the contemporary world."* Then, together with Eric Johnson, our director of public relations and a master symbol-maker, we created a stylized logo for the concept. At the center of the image we placed a lighted lamp of learning, which was intersected by the cross of Christ with its arms and stake reaching out to an ellipse that represented the world. Almost forty years later, the Spring Arbor concept is still intact in word and symbol. Each generation of presidents, students, and faculty has continued to affirm the concept and implement its convictions throughout the curriculum as the school has extended its offerings to graduate and professional degrees, multiplied its enrollment, and become a university. Thanks to Tom Jones, the Spring Arbor concept has the potency of the big idea symbolized by a crisp statement of mission and a logo to match.

Symbols of the Culture

Cultures also use symbols to communicate their differences. Flags of nations become sources of pride for which people will die. Shortly after September 11, 2001, I saw a bumper sticker displaying a picture of the American flag with the words, "These colors do not run." Business mottos can rally the morale of the employees. Peters and Waterman, in their book *In Search of Excellence*, tell about the employee who took the Honda motto of quality so seriously that on the way home from work each evening, he "straightens up windshield wiper blades on all the Hondas he passes. He just can't stand to see a flaw in a Honda!"[2]

Rituals also serve as special symbols to define a culture. Whether it is a national celebration such as a July 4 Independence Day celebration or a local festival such as the county fair, our rituals speak volumes about the character of our culture. As a product of the Midwest, I recall the annual events of "Americana" that drew us together as a community. On these occasions I played first trombone in the high school band, marched to John Philip Sousa, and stood at attention as we played the national anthem and pledged our allegiance to the flag. Although I didn't understand the full meaning of these rites until later, they left me with a sense of roots that our children may not know. Perhaps this childhood heritage is what prompted me to cast the vision for each institution where I served as president in the words of a memorable slogan.

"The Village Is Our Campus." Spring Arbor College (now University) is located at the center of a small village in southern Michigan. A long history of tension between "town and gown" preceded me. Yet, during my graduate study, I had been introduced to a scholar at the University of Chicago named Robert Havinghurst. As part of his theology of Christian education, he said that the institution located in a rural or village setting has a special responsibility for the intellectual, spiritual, and cultural climate of the larger community. Conversely, institutions in an urban environment should capitalize on the intellectual, cultural, and spiritual resources of the city rather than competing with them. Havinghurst's thinking led me to think of Spring Arbor and the surrounding community in the terms, "The village is our classroom." To implement this idea, we sought ways to extend the intellectual, cultural, and spiritual resources of the college to the community through an artist's series, visiting lecturers, spiritual life conferences, athletic events, and other community enrichment programs. Although we never fully closed the gap between the town and the gown, we made progress.

"The City Is Our Campus." At Seattle Pacific College, all systems went into reverse. With the campus located in the heart of a bustling urban area, we would have been foolish to waste resources on duplicating the intellectual, cultural, and spiritual advantages of the metropolis. Instead, we adopted the slogan "The City Is Our Campus" and searched for ways to utilize the wealth of resources around us and also to become engaged with the pains of its poverty. Our goal was to transform the perception that Seattle Pacific College languished as "the little Sunday school by the canal" into the viewpoint that we were partners with the city. We began with the reputation of our teacher education program and entered into dialogue with educators in the African-American community about cooperative

ventures. Reduced-priced tickets to such cultural events as the symphony, opera, and repertory theater were made available to our students. As part of this developing relationship, we found a niche of need in the city for educational enrichment among adults and seniors. Seattle Pacific College was one of the first in the nation to offer a "Senior Learners" program by which our elderly neighbors over 65 could enroll in classes for credit or audit without paying tuition. Soon this program and others were enrolling as many as 2,000 adult learners in what was called the Spiral Program, representing the movement outward from the traditional liberal arts college. Once the perception of our role in the city began to change, we advanced the college to university status in order to express our partnership with other universities in addressing the concerns of the city.

"The World Is Our Parish." Asbury Theological Seminary presented a challenge that fit neither pattern of my past presidencies. The seminary is located in a small village on the edge of Appalachia. After leaving the I-64 or I-75 freeways running through Lexington, Kentucky, a state highway leading south branches into a county road that dead-ends at High Bridge, Kentucky. Two miles down that road is Wilmore, the home of Asbury Theological Seminary and Asbury College. Each new generation of students becomes acquainted with the quip, "Wilmore isn't the end of the earth, but you can see it from there."

Put yourself into that setting as president of the seminary. How do you create a symbol for the vision of Asbury becoming known as a world-class seminary? Our heritage gave us the answer. John Wesley declared, "The world is my parish." Claiming that legacy as Wesleyans, we dared to declare, "The world is our parish." As idealistic as it may sound, the vision energized us to take the lead among seminaries in the fields of lifelong and distance learning. Our imagination sparked again when we remembered John Wesley's conception of his world parish as a "circuit" to be ridden by an army of evangelists on horseback. Although Wesley never heard of the electronic circuitry that we know today, the connection between concepts cannot be denied. If John Wesley were alive today, I have little doubt that his vision of a world parish would be matched by a global system of electronic circuitry. Working with that image, we set up teleconferencing by satellite to sites across the nation for my inauguration as president in 1983. Our alumni and other pastors who gathered at those sites were able to enroll in a continuing education course for ministry, hear Charles Colson give the inaugural lecture, and then participate in the inaugural worship service. Twelve years later, at the time of my retirement, our campus was identified as a "smart" campus with the latest technology for classroom teaching and distance learning. To demonstrate the new reality of our world parish, delegates of the World Methodist Conference participated in two-way interaction with their international president, Dr. Donald English, who spoke to them, saw their faces, and answered their questions from a studio in Leeds, England. On that occasion we literally rode the electronic circuit of our world parish.

Sensitivity to Symbols

Somewhat like an understanding of human history, a leader who fails to learn the culture of an organization will be condemned by it. A couple of examples will illustrate both the success of a leader who paid attention to his culture and the failure of one who did not.

A senior pastor accepted the call to a large metropolitan church with a long history of Swedish ancestry. In fact, after years of offering two Sunday services, one in English and one in Swedish, the Swedish service had just been discontinued. The new pastor came with the handicap of being the first minister without a Swedish background or a Swedish name. His task was to serve a transitional congregation suspended between the past and the present. An early board of trustees meeting brought the issue to a head. The new pastor heard a proposal presented by the building committee for repainting the gymnasium in the bold and striped colors of blue and yellow. "How garish," the pastor immediately thought to himself as the proposal was presented. He was on the verge of speaking his thoughts aloud when a flash of insight crossed his mind: "These are the colors of the Swedish flag." In another flash, he knew that his ministry in the church was "on the line." To oppose the painting would unearth all of the hidden doubts about his ancestry. So, as he told me in confidence, "I bit my tongue and saved my tenure."

On the other side of the ledger, a pastor came to me for counsel after he had failed in his appointment to a large United Methodist church in the South. He inherited a graying congregation. As we talked about the circumstances that led to his dismissal, he mentioned the fact that the former pastor always had a Sunday afternoon service at the local nursing home where so many members chose to live out their days. Almost belligerently he told me, "I will never do this because I have better things to do on Sunday afternoons." In one sentence he arrested, indicted, and convicted himself. Failing to read the cues of the culture, he turned a key symbol of pastoral leadership for that congregation against him. Change was needed, but not without recognizing the strength of the culture that held that congregation together. Nothing else he did regained their confidence. Within a year, he resigned in despair.

Astute leaders are students of culture. They know when to respect its limits and how to introduce change. Cultural symbols, ranging from the colors of a national flag to the ritual of a nursing home visit, serve as tools for their leadership.

Symbols as Tools for Mastery

Human beings make symbols; great leaders master them. Whether it is telling a compelling story to press a point, proposing a logo to communicate a vision, appearing at strategic times and places to illustrate a priority, or making a decision that models the message, leaders of note are gifted symbol-makers.

Britishers were rallied during the siege of London by the sight of Winston Churchill striding over the rubble with the visage of a bulldog accented by a black cigar and a bowler hat. Americans responded with an overwhelming vote to the "V" sign and infectious smile of Dwight Eisenhower. Indians saw Gandhi's message of nonviolence in his emaciated image and simplistic cloak. Black Americans found hope in Martin Luther King Jr.'s genius for turning the phrase, "I have a dream." Germans opened their arms to John F. Kennedy when he began a speech with a simple sentence spoken in their language, "Ich bin ein Berliner." Feminists found their cause in Gloria Steinem's sarcastic simile, "A woman needs a man like a fish needs a bicycle." Ronald Reagan rode roughshod over his critics when he denounced the USSR as the "evil empire."

On the other hand, attempts to use symbols can backfire, particularly among leaders who are perceived to be weak. Gerald Ford provoked laughter with his "WIN" button, and Jimmy Carter lost votes when he tried to reproduce Roosevelt's "Fireside Chats" by appearing before the fireplace dressed in a cardigan sweater. Try as they might, Lyndon Johnson and Richard Nixon never found a captivating symbol around which they could build their presidency. George H. W. Bush never quite made it with his "thousand points of light," and George W. Bush chose the "axis of evil" as a memorable symbol for his administration. Bill Clinton, of course, lost all his symbols of charisma and character in the line by which his presidency will be remembered, "I did not have sexual relations with that woman."

Although less visible and glamorous than the symbols by which national and international leaders are known, the symbols of daily decisions still define the leadership of other executives. On several occasions I have coached prospective and new presidents on setting their inaugural goals, establishing their first priorities, and making their tone-setting decisions. Staff selection often serves as a symbol of leadership. As a coach, my advice is, "Remember that the first person you hire is a symbol that sets the tone and style for your administration." This word of counsel prevents appointments being made too quickly at the sacrifice of quality.

In another coaching session, a presidential prospect called me as he prepared for his interview with the search and selection committee. He had the idea that he would erect a statue of the founding president on the campus mall at the time of his inauguration. I asked him how the statue would symbolize his administration. He went blank and admitted that he wanted to impress the search committee. For an institution that needed turnaround management, such a symbol would surely backfire.

On a more positive note, Bennis and Nanus in their book *Leaders* tell the story of the first decision of a new publisher for the *Los Angeles Herald-Examiner*. Labor versus management conflict had become so intense that the fear of violence caused his predecessor to lock and block the front entrance to the company headquarters. Every employee had to slink around to the back door and go through guards to gain entrance. The new publisher saw the symbol of fear that cowed the employees and made his first decision. He opened and unblocked the front door to let the world know that fear had been dispelled and a new day had dawned.[3]

The Symbol of Strategic Presence

Another bit of counsel that I give to new college and university presidents is to design a plan for what I call "strategic presence." Back in the days of campus protest, a beleaguered president suggested the strategy of getting to know the small core of student leaders very well, listening intently to the larger cohort of leaders, and having a cordial hello for every student on campus. His advice helped me develop my strategy for relating to students on campus. I became intimately acquainted with the core of student leaders, set up informal conversations with a larger group of student leaders, and made sure to greet every student whom I met on the campus. A visit to another campus taught me the value of this strategy as the president and I walked across his campus. I watched as students recognized him and showed the anticipation of a response in their eyes. When he passed by without a look or a word, I knew that he had missed a moment of symbolic command.

Out of this experience I created my own approach to a "strategic presence" on the campus. First I identified the symbolic sites that set the tone and shaped the character of campus life. I saw the chapel as the spiritual center, the library as the intellectual center, the dining commons as the social center, the gymnasium as the physical life center, and the bookstore as the public center.

Because I knew that my schedule would not permit me to be omnipresent on the campus, I chose to be selectively present at each of these strategic places. I never missed chapel when I was on campus, and I scheduled myself to preside or speak on a regular basis. At least once a week I ate in the dining commons with a different group of students. On a regular basis I spent time in the library reading periodicals, researching a subject, and checking out books. During the spring and fall months, I played on the tennis courts, and on a drop-in basis I regularly browsed through the latest publications in the bookstore. Exercising a strategic presence in each of these places, I trusted that the word would spread about my interest in the students and the life of the campus. Although the strategy may sound contrived, it is not. A genuine love for students makes it easy to take the time and enjoy the interaction.

Thirty years later, I received a letter from a former student who had enrolled as an "outsider" to the Christian community of Spring Arbor College. While on campus, however, a life-changing spiritual experience had nudged him into ministry as a military chaplain and Presbyterian pastor. In his letter, Rev. Wayne Rhodes recounts his experiences at Spring Arbor, including these words, "On Sundays I would watch you and your family as you ate with the SAC student body. I was unfamiliar with the real intimacy of a support family. You were an exemplary father and a Christian witness." Needless to say, nothing gives greater gratification than hearing such words.

Leadership literature emphasizes the idea of strategic presence in the acronym M.B.W.A.—for "Management By Walking Around." Fred Smith Sr., another of my mentors in leadership, gives the idea an earthy interpretation when he says, "Nothing grows without fertilizer from the footsteps of the boss." Time and time again, we hear stories about executives who are captives of their office and known to the rank and file of employees only in a formal setting on the boss's turf. In such cases the leadership symbols of time and place are still operative, but the results are negative. "Strategic presence" is one of the most powerful symbols for the exercise of leadership. Those who learn to use it discover that a little time in the right place goes a long way.

We now know why Tom Peters puts heavy emphasis upon symbols as a tool of leadership. Effective leaders will identify the symbols of character, culture, and command in their organizational environment, select those that are most meaningful, and become a master in their exercise.

12

Never Ride
a Pendulum

Like a pendulum that swings from one pole to the opposite, a leader is under constant pressure to take an extreme position or swing between the poles. To succumb to either of these pressures is to forfeit balance and consistency, essential qualities for trust in leadership.

Balancing Vision

Lest anyone forget, leaders are human, and with their humanity comes laughable idiosyncrasies. George Romney, governor of Michigan and presidential aspirant in the 1960s, had a reputation as a hard-charging man with a flash temper. Each morning his office staff awaited his arrival with an alert system to detect the governor's mood for the day. If he arrived in anger because of some issue or person whom he had to confront, word sped through the office network, "The Governor is intense today." Staff members either stayed out of his way or walked gingerly in his presence.

I laughed at the George Romney story until one of my former vice presidents dared to tell me how my staff responded to one of my own leadership quirks. Each Monday morning I held a meeting of the president's cabinet at Asbury Theological Seminary for a report and planning session. Oftentimes I had been away from the campus during the previous week or weekend. The administrative team would always gather early in the outer office with Sheila Lovell, my executive assistant, and ask, "Was the president's plane delayed on the runway yesterday?" If it was, they knew that I'd had extra time to think and plan. Coming into my office, they awaited some fresh idea or new approach related to our mission. The accuracy of their predictions made it a standing joke among them.

It is one thing to be a leader who keeps fresh ideas flowing through the organization and quite another to be one who waffles on the mission to cause anxiety in the community. One of the most visionary and entrepreneurial presidents I know has waffling as his fatal flaw. His administrators and faculty complain that he creates chaos by changing the mission of the institution every six weeks. Tom Peter's book *Thriving on Chaos* is not advocating periodic destruction as a leadership strategy. Rather, he is applauding the merits of leadership that finds direction through the chaos and builds momentum by holding its course. To ride a pendulum on the mission of the organization is to destabilize the system and raise havoc amongst those whom you are called to lead.

Building Trust

Trust is the most precious and precarious relationship between a leader and his followers. It is precious because it cannot be cheapened; it is precarious because it must be earned every day.

I still recall my disillusionment when I visited a longtime friend who had been elected to Congress. He hosted me for lunch in the congressional dining room. For all intents and purposes, he might have been dining all alone. While trying to carry on a conversation, his eyes darted past me to see who was coming into the room. When we finally settled down to lunch, his first question was, "What can I do for you?" Our friendship got lost in the mentality of brokering political power. When this happens, leader and follower are reduced to objects to be used rather than persons to be esteemed or friends to be cherished. Trust that is based upon self-interest is not trust at all. True trust is a bond between people based upon common goals, unbroken integrity, and unconditional self-sacrifice.

Consistency and trust are two sides of the same coin in leadership. Followers, even if fickle themselves, count upon their leaders to hold their course. During the campus protests of the late 1960s, students who dropped out of classes still demanded that they be given credit for their courses with "pass or fail" grades. After the protests passed, a Harvard student came back to her professor with the demand for a letter grade so that she could get into graduate school. Her professor now protested, "When you demanded a 'pass or fail' grade, I gave it to you. Now you are demanding a letter grade. What did you expect me to do?" The student answered, "Just because I panicked, I didn't expect that you would too."

Ronald Reagan gives us the opposite model. After my nomination for secretary of education in his administration, I paid close attention to all of his public pronouncements just in case I had to report directly to him. The results surprised me. I discovered that Ronald Reagan had only one answer to every question. Whatever the context, he reiterated the conservative party line. The more I listened, the better I became at predicting his answers in advance. After a while, the president's responses bordered on creating the boredom of listening to a one-string banjo player. His popularity mystified me until I realized that his consistency won our trust, even if we didn't agree with his politics.

The principle holds for all levels of leadership. Consistency is the quality upon which trust is built. For me, the darkest moments of my administrative career came when the line of trust was either frayed or broken. From these painful moments I adopted a position that I communicated to the faculties of all three institutions where I served as president. Putting my consistency on the line, I made the commitment, "I will do exactly as I have said I will do, and if I change my mind, you will be the first to know." Heads nodded in agreement when I made this pledge, but I still needed to repeat it from time to time. Anyone who leads, even in a Christian community, must earn the trust of followers every day.

Communicating Consistency

Adjectives abound in the description of leadership. We glibly banter about "transformational leadership" and "entrepreneurial leadership." Once in the role, however, glamour gives way to grit. Whether by reengineering or deconstruction, organizational change comes at a price. Noel Tichy and Mary Anne Devanna, in their book *The Transformational Leader*, describe transformational change in three acts: Act I is *Recognizing the Need for Revitalization*; Act II is *Creating a New Vision*; and Act III is *Institutionalizing Change*.[1] Their scenario parallels the same three-act drama posed by William Bridges in his book *Transitions*, where he describes Act I as *Endings*; Act II as *Neutral Zones*; and Act III as *New Beginnings*.[2] In each case, visionary leaders may be adept at seeing Old Endings for an organization that needs to be transformed. Others may be skilled in implementing New Beginnings in the organizational structure. The transformational drama, however, is not complete without Act II, the time of Transition between Old Endings and

New Beginnings, when the future of the organization hangs in the balance. During this time anxiety reigns among those whose lives are affected by the circumstances of change over which they have no control. Only the consistency of commitment on the part of the leader keeps the transformational drama from falling apart.

Two of the most gifted leaders I know have histories of leading organizations into Act I of the transformational drama with its emphasis upon ending the old and starting the new. But then, with Act II, the Transition, barely under way, they left for other posts in which they could start the drama all over again. They took trust with them. Those who followed inherited a climate of chaos in the organization and confusion among the membership.

No organization can be transformed without a leader who envisions change, points out the destination, and holds the course. The challenge is comparable to a parent's role during a child's adolescence. Although it may appear as if the adolescent is rebelling against all of the rules and values set by the parent, the fact is that the child is sharpening his or her individual identity against the parental standards. Unless the parent remains consistent in holding those standards, the adolescent becomes confused by the blurring of the lines. Nothing is worse than parental conflict or vacillation over those standards. If one parent is overly strict and the other is unduly soft, the tragic result can be a child without a clear social conscience or moral identity.

The analogy applies to organizations in transition as well. Like an adolescent, an organization cannot go through the storm and stress of change and develop its new identity without a leader who keeps the vision clear and holds the course during the time of change. A leader who rides a pendulum during the time of transition blurs the vision, loses trust, and aborts the transformational drama.

Handling Ambiguity

A swinging pendulum also describes the environment within which leaders must work. Opposite poles represent the paradox that defines the leader's task. The space between is a no-man's-land, characterized by conflict and filled with ambiguity.

Our two sons are organizational psychologists. After studying many theories of leadership, they have concluded that a leader who best handles paradox stands out above the rest. Douglas, our oldest son, coaches Microsoft executives with his "C-2" theory. One "C" stands for "conviction," the other relates to "connection." In simple terms, it means that an executive who can make a decision based upon conviction or principle without losing connection with people is performing with distinction as a leader. Our younger son, Rob, puts the same paradox in terms used by Edward Friedman in his description of a "self-differentiated" leader. In this case, a "sense of self" must be balanced by a "sense of others." A self-differentiated leader walks a tightrope between these extremes. The opposites may be clear, but ambiguity rules the ground in the middle. Also, saboteurs within the organization are constantly at work trying to push the leader to one extreme or the other. If the saboteurs win, self-differentiation is lost.

Imagine an executive decision involving this kind of paradox with ambiguity in the middle. Whenever I think back upon the decisions I made as a president, I remember the dilemma of dealing with issues of tension between my responsibility for the institution and my responsibility for an individual. A painful decision comes to mind. In one institution where I served, information came to me that a tenured professor was killing a popular major because students felt cheated in class. Thirty-five or more students enrolled in the introductory class, but that number dwindled to a dozen at the semester, and it ended with only three to five students in the advanced class. I also learned that the teacher exhibited paranoid symptoms by browbeating students and accusing them of conspiracy. Colleagues in the faculty joined with students in their protest.

The president's paradox is obvious in this case. I was caught between my responsibility for the individual and my responsibility to the institution. Compounding the dilemma, I had to deal with a tenured professor who had taught a lifetime in the institution. To dismiss a tenured professor would invoke the wrath of the American Association of University Professors. To discipline or dismiss a longtime member of the faculty without explanation would rouse the sentiments of community. Yet I could not ignore my commitment to academic quality in our classes or forfeit my responsibility for student confidence in our faculty. Adding to the complexity, when the dean informed the professor of student dissatisfaction, the paranoia checked in and a lawsuit was threatened. Knowing that tenure can only be revoked for insanity, immorality, or incompetence, I realized how difficult it is to prove any one of the three beyond reasonable doubt.

Still, I had no choice. My institutional obligation required action. With Ken Blanchard's adage from *The One Minute Manager* in mind, I had to try to "eliminate the behavior and keep the person."[3] It did not work. When the dean recommended dismissal with continuation of pay until the age of early retirement, the professor demanded a grievance hearing. At the mention of a hearing, however, all of the faculty and student accusers refused to appear. The dean was left stranded without support for his recommendation. Of course, this deepened the dilemma because I now had to make a decision that affected the dean's credibility.

I could see no way out until we remembered a provision in the rights and responsibilities of educational institutions called "financial exigency." The provision permitted us to cut a major field of study whose enrollment showed a precipitous drop into a deep deficit. On the negative side, we could not offer the same major for at least five years after discontinuation. Ultimately, I made the decision to cut the major, provide generous severance pay and counseling for the ineffective faculty member, and reassign the other faculty. While avoiding legal suits, I sacrificed a popular major for a five-year period. As all readers will quickly note, I made a decision with "the proportions veiled in mist." There were no winners, and Monday morning quarterbacks had a heyday. Trying to keep my sense of humor, I concluded that the decision must be good because I had made everybody mad. Such is the life of a leader. Paradox is the raw material for our labor, ambiguity is our working environment, and compromise that balances institutional and individual interests is our product.

Parker Palmer gives the paradox a deeply moving, spiritual cast in his book *Let Your Life Speak*.[4] He writes, "The deepest vocational question is not 'What ought I to do with my life?' It is the more elemental and demanding, 'Who am I? What is my nature?'" In every decision, a leader is suspended on the horns of the dilemma posed by these questions. Our sense of being is found in the answer to the question, "Who am I?" and our sense of belonging comes with the answer to the question, "Whose am I?" Christian leaders have common answers to these questions. Our sense of being comes with the incarnational promise of "Christ in us," and our sense of belonging is given with the witness of the Spirit that we are a "child of God."

Until we answer the deepest of these vocational questions for ourselves, we will ride the pendulum between extremes and resolve nothing. But if we know *who we are* and *to whom we belong*, we will be able to work through ambiguity to achieve a measure of balance in our leadership.

13

Never Expect Thanks

In Max DePree's three-part definition of leadership, he says, "The first responsibility is to define reality, the last is to say 'Thank you.' In between, a leader must be a debtor and a servant of all."[1] A corollary to this definition might be, "Always say 'thanks,' but never expect it."

Thanks—A Leader's Gift

Saying "Thank you" does not come naturally for most leaders. After assigning a task or delegating a responsibility, a leader expects results without adulation. A tale is told about a Native American chief who won a court ruling over the rights to land claimed by his forefathers. With pomp and circumstance, government officers made the transition ceremony a major celebration. When it came time for the chief to respond on behalf of his tribe, he accepted the deed with a grunt and walked away. Federal dignitaries showed their shock and accused the chief of being rude and ungrateful. A wise bystander, however, who understood the chief's mind, offered the explanation, "Why should he say 'Thank you' for something that already belonged to him?"

Executive leaders may wish that they could take the same attitude toward employees who are just doing their job, but they cannot. The boss's "Thank you" aptly given is a key to motivation and morale. When executives overdo their thanks, the gesture loses meaning. Those who find "Thanks" stuck in their throats like Macbeth's "Amen" miss a golden moment. In between the extremes, a word of gratitude for an accomplished task, an extra effort, a show of loyalty, or a sign of personal caring establishes a bond which gains strength and pays dividends over time. People often say that a leader does not care who gets the credit as long as the task is done and the goal is reached. These are idle words if a leader takes all of the credit by failing to say "Thanks" to his or her followers both personally and publicly. The ability to say "Thanks" may well be one of the characteristics that defines greatness in leadership.

Thanks—A Leader's Tool

A leader is often overburdened with unresolved issues that percolate up through the system. Whether they realize it or not, subordinates often add to the overload by "bucking up" sensitive or controversial matters to their superior and leaving them there. In my case, I often told my subordinates to take the issue, make a decision, and report back to me. As a way of reinforcing this action and easing my overload, I made it a special point to say thank you to people who dealt directly with problems at the level of their responsibility. A simple word of gratitude confirmed their authority and my confidence. It also served as a tool for leadership. Subordinates soon learned that they could not bypass middle management and take their problems directly to the top.

Having served as a middle manager before assuming executive leadership, I especially understand middle managers' feeling about being torn between the top and the bottom. They must operate in the contested territory between a chief executive officer who feels overburdened and a staff who feels abandoned. They are expected to be loyal to both parties and juggle their decisions in the balance of both interests. To say thank you to these beleaguered middle managers for living with these pressures usually comes as a surprise to them. "Thank you" is a way of letting them know that their leader understands how they are torn and cares about their tension.

Staff members are most needy for a word of thanks. Their ranks encompass a wide range of support functions that includes everything from high-tech services to custodial services. No one doubts that staff people carry a workload that makes or breaks an organization at a foundational level. Yet they often fail to receive their proportionate share of the credit. A spontaneous word of thanks in a nonformal setting is a cure for abandonment and an elixir for any symptoms of self-doubt.

James March and Michael Cohen, in their book *Leadership and Ambiguity: The American College President*, observe that hospitals and universities are similar organizations in having an informal caste system based upon professional credentials.[2] When I took my clinical residency at a university hospital in order to be credentialed as a chaplain, I learned firsthand what March and Cohen mean. During the first two weeks of my training, I had to serve as an orderly without anyone knowing that I had a graduate degree in psychology or the credentials of ministerial ordination. My green orderly's jacket put me at the lowest level of the hospital hierarchy. From this position I learned about professional prejudice from the bottom up. A licensed practical nurse told me that as an orderly, I would soon know the name and number of every bedpan in my ward. The licensed practical nurses, however, took orders from the registered nurses, who obeyed the general practitioners, who bowed to the surgeons and psychiatrists. Except for hearing sharp commands from those immediately above me, I felt like a nonentity. The scene was reminiscent of the New England adage, "The Cabots speak only to the Lodges, and the Lodges speak only to God." If anyone said "Thank you" to me as an orderly, it was an aberration. Within that two-week period, I felt as one with friends working at minimum wage. They starved for a word of recognition and a gesture of thanks.

Years later, as a college president, I observed a similar caste system at work in higher education. Beneath the surface of an alleged collegiality, an underlying labor versus management mentality drew a Maginot Line between administrators and faculty. This attitude surfaced one day after I had appointed the leading spokesperson for the faculty to a deanship. In the very next faculty meeting, his professorial peers denied him a vote in their deliberations because he had shifted sides even while retaining his faculty rank and status.

Administrators learn to deal with this divided company as a matter of course, but staff members have neither the position nor the power to handle their slights. When I first read the theory that staff members in an organization felt as if they were abandoned, I thought that the case had been overstated. I was wrong. Once I began to observe the interaction between people at different strata on the academic totem pole, I knew why staff members felt abandoned. Faculty members can become so involved in the esoteric nature of their fields of study that they forget the importance of the support systems that attract and retain students for their classes. By and large, staff members for admissions, financial aid, student life, and the library, along with such services as dining and maintenance, are not appreciated for the role they play in assuring a quality institution. As a partial remedy for this unfair situation, I instituted several changes. One was to give my annual state of the institution address before the whole community so that faculty and staff joined as one to hear the vision renewed and see their role in the implementation of that mission. In another deliberate move, I went to staff meetings just as I did faculty meetings to give a president's report and commend the staff for their work. These formal connections were reinforced by more personalized actions. By presiding at annual functions of staff orientation and consecration services, hosting the Christmas party and award luncheons, and dropping in on staff coffee hours and birthday parties, I let my presence say "Thanks." Most important of all, my wife and I made it a point to know staff members by name and thank them personally whenever they served or helped us. To return to the campus now is to renew acquaintance with lasting friends among both faculty and staff. A word of thanks, judiciously given, is far more than a leader's last responsibility. It is a special privilege that goes with the role.

Thanks—A Leader's Need

Our story has another side. While leaders have the responsibility and privilege to say "Thank you," they cannot expect the same in return. Sometimes it seems as if followers have a silent conspiracy based on the code, "Never say thanks to the boss." Perhaps this reflects the idea that subordinates should always be pressing leaders with the question, "What have you done for me today?" Or it may come from the fear that "Thank you" represents a concession to authority with the motive of seeking further favors. Whatever it is, a leader who needs a "Thank you" from followers as affirmation for well-being is bound to be disenchanted. Leadership has its own rewards, but "Thank you" from followers is not usually one of them. Just as a leader must bite bullets on tough decisions, he or she must also count on an undaunted commitment to a mission to provide its own affirmation.

For years the lack of spontaneous thanks from followers bothered me. No matter how I struggled to balance budgets and keep faculty salaries rising, I never heard a word of gratitude. My frustration showed one day when I blurted out, "If only they would say 'thanks' just once, it would all be worth it!" Such self-pity is also self-defeating. Not until the very end of my career did I hear those long-awaited words. After receiving a multi-million dollar grant, we bought personal computers for every faculty member. In the next faculty meeting, a junior professor spoke up to say, "I think that we should say 'thank you' to the administration for this gift." As small as the incident seems, it still sticks out in my mind.

Retirement has taught me the greater lesson. Sometimes the cycle of a full generation must pass before followers can say "Thank you" to a leader. Now when I return to the campus settings where I served, former antagonists are among my most appreciative friends. At first I thought, "Why didn't you show some gratitude when we worked together?" When I shared this dilemma with my wife, her wisdom supplied the answer: "Maybe their silence was a sign of their confidence in you. Maybe you sharpened each other." Her words took me to Proverbs 27:17, "As iron sharpens iron, so one man sharpens another." This is the nature of the academic community and many other organizations. Appreciation comes with confidence in the competence of the leader. Even in vigorous debate that whets the edge of intellect and hones the focus of mission of the institution, a measure of appreciation can be implied. Mutual respect is a silent word of thanks.

Surprising Thanks—A Leader's Reward

If I were asked to note one of the highlights of my life, I would cite the 30th anniversary of the 1972 graduating class of Seattle Pacific University. When I accepted the presidency of Seattle Pacific in 1968, my wife and I identified with the freshman class and went through orientation with them. Four years later they graduated, but we stayed for another ten years. So when the class celebrated its 30th reunion in 2002, they invited us to meet with them as classmates. Little did we know what the evening would hold.

After the typical introductions and pleasantries, I was asked to share some memories with the class and personalize our journey into retirement. Following my comments, the master of ceremonies asked members of the class to speak their memories. I could not believe what I heard. Taking the cue from my reflections, two alumni mentioned the times when they had been in my office for discipline. One was the editor of the student newspaper, whom I fired, and another had been guilty of a dangerous prank. I assumed that they still held a grudge because of my administrative decisions that punished them. But instead they thanked me for taking disciplinary action that directly influenced their character and their success. As if wonders never cease, still another two or three remembered chapel addresses I had given that had a direct effect upon shaping their Christian character. In one instance I had written off the chapel address as a "bomb." Little did I know how the Holy Spirit used my sense of failure for his glory. I had thought that no one was listening.

Most surprising of all, the alumni remembered the financial crisis we were going through during their student days thirty-some years earlier. Heads nodded in affirmation when one of the grads spoke to me, "We know that you were under great financial pressure during those years, but thanks for holding steady and getting the institution back on its feet." I could hardly believe my ears. Not only did the students know that I carried the burden of leadership, but they cared. In that instant my whole career flashed before my eyes and I felt a gratifying sense of worth—all due to former students who said "Thank you." A leader's trophies are not etched on brass; they are written in flesh.

14

Free Indeed!

L eaders work within more constraints than we think. The *legal constraints* are well known. Whether in a public or private organization, a leader cannot exceed the boundaries of the corporate charter, federal guidelines, state regulations, and local ordinances. A public college president once told me that legal restraints of this nature were so limiting that he had only 5 percent margins within which to leverage his leadership.

On top of the legal restraints, a leader must work within the limits of *governance constraints*, which include policies, precedents, and procedures of the organization itself. A policy requiring that the chief executive officer present a balanced budget to the governing board is an example of these limits. Further, discipline is found in the leader's job description, which sets the expectations for character and competence as well as lists the outcomes for performance. When a chief executive officer is identified as the sole employee of the governing board, for instance, it does not mean that he or she can function with the freedom of a Lone Ranger. Quite to the contrary. Sole executive authority also means sole staff responsibility, and with it comes a limit on freedom. Add then the *cultural constraints* of unwritten mores, norms, customs, and rituals, which can be equally binding on a leader. As we noted earlier, success or failure can pivot on the extent to which a leader is sensitive to the dotted lines on the map of the internal culture and external environment. Although these limits when listed may seem onerous, they are not. Like the proverbial river that flows fast and deep within its banks, an effective leader finds leverage within limits for creative action.

The greater discipline comes from deep within the leader. *Moral constraints* that define action in gray areas of entrepreneurial risk or ethical question belong to the leader alone. We honor the individual who errs on the side of caution when moral decisions are involved. The courage to say, "I don't feel right about it" when all of the systems say "Go" is a quality of leadership that also defines character. Even more, a leader who acts within *spiritual constraints* will stand out as a model for all of us. The discipline of God's will may provoke a skeptical laugh in some sectors, but Christian leaders are distinguished by the fact that they serve within those limits.

The Heartbeat of Freedom

In this book we have been exploring another limit on leadership. Intuition and experience come into play when we use the term "Never" as a boundary that sets the leader free. Although this freedom is inferred in each of the chapters of the book, now we can think more specifically about the "GO" that comes when we say "NO."

True freedom for leadership is not unbridled license. Like the human heartbeat, freedom to lead has two strokes in the cycle—"freedom *from*" something that is self-destructive and "freedom *to*" be someone who is self-giving. We see this heartbeat in each of McKenna's Maxims:

Never play God frees us
  from: pride in our position
  to: lead with CREATIVITY
Never blink in a hailstorm frees us
  from: cowardice under pressure
  to: lead with CONSISTENCY
Never go solo frees us
  from: betraying our trust
  to: lead with ACCOUNTABILITY
Never steal a paper clip frees us
  from: fearing exposure
  to: lead with INTEGRITY
Never swallow perfume frees us
  from: falling for flattery
  to: lead with HUMILITY
Never build without a balcony frees us
  from: making regrettable decisions
  to: lead with PERSPECTIVE
Never waste an interruption frees us
  from: being enslaved by schedules
  to: lead with SPONTANEITY
Never die from failure frees us
  from: dreading a risk
  to: lead by LEARNING
Never hide behind a gas mask frees us
  from: avoiding confrontation
  to: lead with CONVICTION
Never sniff at symbols frees us
  from: fear of imagination
  to: lead with ARTISTRY

Never ride a pendulum frees us
 from: paralysis at extremes
 to: lead with BALANCE
Never expect thanks frees us
 from: overdependence upon affirmation
 to: lead with SELF-WORTH

So when all is said and done, we who lead are liberated by our own discipline. Rather than depending upon others to draw the boundaries within which we find our freedom, we can draw those boundaries from the lessons of experience. Certainly every leader wants to report to a governing body that says, "GO until we say STOP." These are liberating words for any leader. Within these broad boundaries, however, are the self-imposed disciplines of leadership. While working through these limits, we will discover the greater freedom implied in the apparent paradox, "When NO means GO." Formal boundaries give us freedom of function, but informal boundaries open up dimensions of freedom that are moral and spiritual in character. Despite all the emphasis upon leadership in every sector of society, this is still a missing dimension. Courses in ethics, seminars in team building, or formulas for leadership development do not fill the gap. Perhaps now is the time to give the lessons of experience a try. The leader who exercises the self-discipline of serving within moral and spiritual boundaries will be free—free indeed!

Notes

Chapter 1: When "No" Means "Go"

1. Max DePree, *Leadership Is an Art* (New York: Bantam Doubleday Dell, 1989).
2. John Carver, *Boards That Make a Difference*, 2d ed. (San Francisco: Jossey-Bass, 1997), 79–82.
3. Ibid., 74–100.
4. John W. Gardner, *Excellence* (New York: W. W. Norton, 1984), 86.
5. Oren Harari, *The Leadership Secrets of Colin Powell* (New York: McGraw-Hill, 2002), 13.
6. Quoted in L. I. Ponomarev, *The Quantum Dice* (Moscow: Mir Publishers, 1988), http://www.gap.dcs.st-and.ac.uk/~history/Quotations/Bohr_Niels.html.

Chapter 2: Never Play God

1. Philip Evans and Thomas S. Wurster, *Blown to Bits* (Boston: Harvard Business School Press, 2000), 23–38.
2. Henri J. M. Nouwen, *In the Name of Jesus* (New York: Crossroad, 1991), 35.
3. Ibid.
4. Ibid., 55–70.

Chapter 4: Never Go Solo

1. Nouwen, *In the Name of Jesus*, 35–39.
2. Ibid., 41.
3. Robert Townsend, *Up the Organization* (New York: Alfred A. Knopf, 1970), 85.

Chapter 5: Never Steal a Paper Clip

1. Quoted in "Nixon's Ghost," *Christianity Today*, April 22, 2002, 24.
2. Ibid.
3. Richard Foster, *Money, Sex, and Power* (San Francisco: Harper & Row, 1985).
4. Nouwen, *In the Name of Jesus*, 35–51.

Chapter 7: Never Build without a Balcony

1. William Ury, *Getting Past No: Negotiating with Difficult People* (New York: Penguin Books, 1991).
2. Ibid., 12.
3. Ibid., 8–9.
4. Ibid., 29–32.

Chapter 8: Never Waste an Interruption

1. Henri J. M. Nouwen, *Reaching Out* (Garden City, NY: Doubleday, 1966).
2. Terence R. Mitchell and James R. Larson Jr., *People in Organizations: An Introduction to Organizational Behavior*, 3d ed. (New York: McGraw-Hill, 1982), 480.
3. Ibid.

Chapter 9: Never Die from Failure

1. Warren Bennis and Burt Nanus, *Leaders: Four Strategies for Taking Charge* (New York: Harper & Row, 1985), 70.
2. Steven Hayward, *Churchill on Leadership* (Rocklin, CA: Prima Publishing, 1997), 29.

3. Arnold Blomberg, *Great Leaders, Great Tyrants?* (Westport, CT: Greenwood, 1995).

4. William Gates, *Business @ the Speed of Thought* (New York: Warner Books, 1999), 262–269.

5. Howard Gardner, *Leading Minds: An Anatomy of Leadership* (New York: Basic Books, 1995).

6. Ibid., 290.

7. Ibid.

8. Ibid., 307–325.

9. Bennis and Nanus, 69.

10. Ibid.

11. Ibid., 72.

12. Gates, 184.

13. Ibid., 184–185.

14. Bennis and Nanus, 69–79.

Chapter 10: Never Hide behind a Gas Mask

1. Edwin H. Friedman, *Generation to Generation: Family Process in Church and Synagogue* (New York: Guilford Press, 1985).

Chapter 11: Never Sniff at Symbols

1. Thomas J. Peters and Robert H. Waterman, *In Search of Excellence: Lessons from America's Best-Run Companies* (New York: Harper & Row, 1982), xvii–xxvi.

2. Ibid., 37.

3. Bennis and Nanus, 37–39.

Chapter 12: Never Ride a Pendulum

1. Noel Tichy and Mary Anne Devanna, *The Transformational Leader* (New York: John Wiley and Sons, 1986), 5–6.

2. Ibid., 32–33.

3. Ken Blanchard and Spencer Johnson, *The One Minute Manager* (New York: William Morrow/Harper Collins Publishers, Inc., 1981), 82.

4. Parker Palmer, *Let Your Life Speak* (San Francisco: Jossey-Bass, 2000), 15–17.

Chapter 13: Never Expect Thanks

1. Max DePree, *Leadership Is an Art*, 11.

2. James G. March and Michael D. Cohen, *Leadership and Ambiguity: The American College President* (New York: McGraw-Hill Book Co., 1974), 81.

David L. McKenna was thirty years old when he became the youngest college president in the nation. He went on to serve as president of many other colleges and seminaries, including Seattle Pacific University and Asbury Theological Seminary. He has studied leadership principles all his life and continues, in retirement, in consulting roles. He lives in Sammamish, Washington.